The Ultimate
ECAA Guide

Published by *RAR Medical Services Limited*
www.uniadmissions.co.uk
info@uniadmissions.co.uk
Tel: 0208 068 0438

The Ultimate ECAA Guide

300 Practice Questions

David Meacham
Rohan Agarwal

UniAdmissions

About the Authors

David is a **Merger & Acquisitions Associate** at The Hut Group, a leading online retailer and brand owner in the Beauty & Wellness sectors. Prior to joining The Hut Group, he worked in roles at the Professional Service firm Deloitte, the Investment Bank Greenhill and the Private Equity firm Hgcapital.

David graduated with a **first class honours** in Economics from Gonville and Caius College Cambridge, where he received two college scholarships for outstanding academic performance, in addition to an Essay Prize. He is also a qualified accountant and chartered tax adviser, passing all exams first-time with multiple regional top scores. Since graduating, David has tutored & successfully provided academic coaching to hundreds of students, both in a personal capacity and for university admissions.

Rohan is the **Director of Operations** at *UniAdmissions* and is responsible for its technical and commercial arms. He graduated from Gonville and Caius College, Cambridge and is a fully qualified doctor. Over the last five years, he has tutored hundreds of successful Oxbridge and Medical applicants. He has also authored ten books on admissions tests and interviews.

Rohan has taught physiology to undergraduates and interviewed medical school applicants for Cambridge. He has published research on bone physiology and writes education articles for the Independent and Huffington Post. In his spare time, Rohan enjoys playing the piano and table tennis.

The Basics

What is the ECAA?
The Economics Admissions Assessment (ECAA) is a two hour written exam for prospective Cambridge Economics applicants.

What does the ECAA consist of?

Section	SKILLS TESTED	Questions	Timing
1A	Problem-solving	20 MCQs	80 minutes
1B	Advanced Mathematics	15 MCQs	
2	Writing Task	One Long Essay	40 minutes

Why is the ECAA used?
Cambridge applicants tend to be a bright bunch and therefore usually have excellent grades. The majority of economics applicants score in excess of 90% in their A level subjects. This means that competition is fierce – meaning that the universities must use the ECAA to help differentiate between applicants.

When do I sit ECAA?
The ECAA normally takes place in the first week of November every year, normally on a Wednesday Morning.

Can I resit the ECAA?
No, you can only sit the ECAA once per admissions cycle.

Where do I sit the ECAA?
You can usually sit the ECAA at your school or college (ask your exams officer for more information). Alternatively, if your school isn't a registered test centre or you're not attending a school or college, you can sit the ECAA at an authorised test centre.

Who has to sit the ECAA?
All applicants for Cambridge Economics need to sit the test.

Do I have to resit the ECAA if I reapply?
Yes, each admissions cycle is independent - you cannot use your score from any previous attempts.

How is the ECAA Scored?
In section 1, each question carries one mark and there is no negative marking. Both sections 1A + 1B are equally weighted. In section 2, your answer will be assessed based on the argument and also its clarity.

How is the ECAA used?
Different Cambridge colleges will place different weightings on different components so its important you find out as much information about how your marks will be used by emailing the college admissions office.

In general, the university will interview a high proportion of realitstic applicants so the ECAA score isn't vital for making the interview shortlist. However, it can play a huge role in the final decision after your interview

General Advice

Start Early

It is much easier to prepare if you practice little and often. Start your preparation well in advance; ideally by mid September but at the latest by early October. This way you will have plenty of time to complete as many papers as you wish to feel comfortable and won't have to panic and cram just before the test, which is a much less effective and more stressful way to learn. In general, an early start will give you the opportunity to identify the complex issues and work at your own pace.

Prioritise

Some questions in sections 1 + 2 can be long and complex – and given the intense time pressure you need to know your limits. It is essential that you don't get stuck with very difficult questions. If a question looks particularly long or complex, mark it for review and move on. You don't want to be caught 5 questions short at the end just because you took more than 3 minutes in answering a challenging multi-step physics question. If a question is taking too long, choose a sensible answer and move on. Remember that each question carries equal weighting and therefore, you should adjust your timing in accordingly. With practice and discipline, you can get very good at this and learn to maximise your efficiency.

Positive Marking

There are no penalties for incorrect answers in the ECAA; you will gain one for each right answer and will not get one for each wrong or unanswered one. This provides you with the luxury that you can always guess should you absolutely be not able to figure out the right answer for a question or run behind time. Since each question provides you with 4 to 6 possible answers, you have a 16-25% chance of guessing correctly. Therefore, if you aren't sure (and are running short of time), then make an educated guess and move on. Before 'guessing' you should try to eliminate a couple of answers to increase your chances of getting the question correct. For example, if a question has 5 options and you manage to eliminate 2 options- your chances of getting the question increase from 20% to 33%!

Avoid losing easy marks on other questions because of poor exam technique. Similarly, if you have failed to finish the exam, take the last 10 seconds to guess the remaining questions to at least give yourself a chance of getting them right.

Practice

This is the best way of familiarising yourself with the style of questions and the timing for this section. Although the ECAA tests only GCSE level knowledge, you are unlikely to be familiar with the style of questions in all 3 sections when you first encounter them. Therefore, you want to be comfortable at using this before you sit the test.

Practising questions will put you at ease and make you more comfortable with the exam. The more comfortable you are, the less you will panic on the test day and the more likely you are to score highly. Initially, work through the questions at your own pace, and spend time carefully reading the questions and looking at any additional data. When it becomes closer to the test, **make sure you practice the questions under exam conditions**.

Past Papers

The ECAA is a very new exam so there aren't many sample papers available. Specimen papers are freely available online at www.uniadmissions.co.uk/ECAA. Once you've worked your way through the questions in this book, you are highly advised to attempt them.

Repeat Questions

When checking through answers, pay particular attention to questions you have got wrong. If there is a worked answer, look through that carefully until you feel confident that you understand the reasoning, and then repeat the question without help to check that you can do it. If only the answer is given, have another look at the question and try to work out why that answer is correct. This is the best way to learn from your mistakes, and means you are less likely to make similar mistakes when it comes to the test. The same applies for questions which you were unsure of and made an educated guess which was correct, even if you got it right. When working through this book, **make sure you highlight any questions you are unsure of**, this means you know to spend more time looking over them once marked.

Top tip! In general, students tend to improve the fastest in section 2 and slowest in section 1A; section 1B usually falls somewhere in the middle. Thus, if you have very little time left, it's best to prioritise section 2.

No Calculators

You aren't permitted to use calculators in the ECAA – thus, it is essential that you have strong numerical skills. For instance, you should be able to rapidly convert between percentages, decimals and fractions. You will seldom get questions that would require calculators but you would be expected to be able to arrive at a sensible estimate. Consider for example:

Estimate 3.962 x 2.322;

3.962 is approximately 4 and 2.323 is approximately 2.33 = 7/3.

Thus, $$3.962 \, x \, 2.322 \approx 4 \, x\frac{7}{3} = \frac{28}{3} = 9.33$$

Since you will rarely be asked to perform difficult calculations, you can use this as a signpost of if you are tackling a question correctly. For example, when solving a physics question, you end up having to divide 8,079 by 357- this should raise alarm bells as calculations in the ECAA are rarely this difficult.

A word on timing...

"If you had all day to do your ECAA, you would get 100%. But you don't."

Whilst this isn't completely true, it illustrates a very important point. Once you've practiced and know how to answer the questions, the clock is your biggest enemy. This seemingly obvious statement has one very important consequence. **The way to improve your ECAA score is to improve your speed.** There is no magic bullet. But there are a great number of techniques that, with practice, will give you significant time gains, allowing you to answer more questions and score more marks.

Timing is tight throughout the ECAA – **mastering timing is the first key to success.** Some candidates choose to work as quickly as possible to save up time at the end to check back, but this is generally not the best way to do it. ECAA questions can have a lot of information in them – each time you start answering a question it takes time to get familiar with the instructions and information. By splitting the question into two sessions (the first run-through and the return-to-check) you double the amount of time you spend on familiarising yourself with the data, as you have to do it twice instead of only once. This costs valuable time. In addition, candidates who do check back may spend 2–3 minutes doing so and yet not make any actual changes. Whilst this can be reassuring, it is a false reassurance as it is unlikely to have a significant effect on your actual score. Therefore it is usually best to pace yourself very steadily, aiming to spend the same amount of time on each question and finish the final question in a section just as time runs out. This reduces the time spent on re-familiarising with questions and maximises the time spent on the first attempt, gaining more marks.

It is essential that you don't get stuck with the hardest questions – no doubt there will be some. In the time spent answering only one of these you may miss out on answering three easier questions. If a question is taking too long, choose a sensible answer and move on. Never see this as giving up or in any way failing, rather it is the smart way to approach a test with a tight time limit. With practice and discipline, you can get very good at this and learn to maximise your efficiency. It is not about being a hero and aiming for full marks – this is almost impossible and very much unnecessary (even Oxbridge will regard any score higher than 7 as exceptional). It is about maximising your efficiency and gaining the maximum possible number of marks within the time you have.

> *Top tip!* Ensure that you take a watch that can show you the time in seconds into the exam. This will allow you have a much more accurate idea of the time you're spending on a question. In general, if you've spent more than 3 minutes on question – move on regardless of how close you think you are to solving it.

Use the Options:

Some questions may try to overload you with information. When presented with large tables and data, it's essential you look at the answer options so you can focus your mind. This can allow you to reach the correct answer a lot more quickly. Consider the example below:

The table below shows the results of a study investigating antibiotic resistance in staphylococcus populations. A single staphylococcus bacterium is chosen at random from a similar population. Resistance to any one antibiotic is independent of resistance to others.

Calculate the probability that the bacterium selected will be resistant to all four drugs.

A   1 in 10^6
B   1 in 10^{12}
C   1 in 10^{20}
D   1 in 10^{25}
E   1 in 10^{30}
F   1 in 10^{35}

Antibiotic	Number of Bacteria tested	Number of Resistant Bacteria
Benzyl-penicillin	10^{11}	98
Chloramphenicol	10^9	1200
Metronidazole	10^8	256
Erythromycin	10^5	2

Looking at the options first makes it obvious that there is **no need to calculate exact values**- only in powers of 10. This makes your life a lot easier. If you hadn't noticed this, you might have spent well over 90 seconds trying to calculate the exact value when it wasn't even being asked for.

In other cases, you may actually be able to use the options to arrive at the solution quicker than if you had tried to solve the question as you normally would. Consider the example below:

A region is defined by the two inequalities: $x - y^2 > 1 \: and \: xy > 1$. Which of the following points is in the defined region?

A. (10,3)
B. (10,2)
C. (-10,3)
D. (-10,2)
E. (-10,-3)

Whilst it's possible to solve this question both algebraically or graphically by manipulating the identities, by far **the quickest way is to actually use the options**. Note that options C, D and E violate the second inequality, narrowing down to answer to either A or B. For A: $10 - 3^2 = 1$ and thus this point is on the boundary of the defined region and not actually in the region. Thus the answer is B (as $10-4 = 6 > 1$.)

In general, it pays dividends to look at the options briefly and see if they can be help you arrive at the question more quickly. Get into this habit early – it may feel unnatural at first but it's guaranteed to save you time in the long run.

Keywords

If you're stuck on a question; pay particular attention to the options that contain key modifiers like "**always**", "**only**", "**all**" as examiners like using them to test if there are any gaps in your knowledge. E.g. the statement "arteries carry oxygenated blood" would normally be true; "All arteries carry oxygenated blood" would be false because the pulmonary artery carries deoxygenated blood.

SECTION 1

This is the first section of the ECAA and as you walk in, it is inevitable that you will feel nervous. Make sure that you have been to the toilet because once it starts you cannot simply pause and go. Take a few deep breaths and calm yourself down. Remember that panicking will not help and may negatively affect your marks- so try and avoid this as much as possible.

You have one hour to answer 35 questions in section 1. Whilst this section of the ECAA is renowned for being difficult to prepare for, there are powerful shortcuts and techniques that you can use to save valuable time on these types of questions.

You have just above 2 minutes per question; this may sound like a lot but given that you're often required to analyse passages or graphs- it can often not be enough. Some questions in this section are very tricky and can be a big drain on your limited time. **The people who fail to complete section 1 are those who get bogged down on a particular question**.

Therefore, it is vital that you start to get a feel for which questions are going to be easy and quick to do and which ones should be left till the end. The best way to do this is through practice and the questions in this book will offer extensive opportunities for you to do so.

SECTION 1A: Problem Solving Questions

Section 1 problem solving questions are arguably the hardest to prepare for. However, there are some useful techniques you can employ to solve some types of questions much more quickly:

Construct Equations

Some of the problems in Section 1 are quite complex and you'll need to be comfortable with turning prose into equations and manipulating them. For example, when you read "Mark is twice as old as Jon" – this should immediately register as M = 2J. Once you get comfortable forming equations, you can start to approach some of the harder questions in this book (and past papers) which may require you to form and solve simultaneous equations. Consider the example:

Nick has a sleigh that contains toy horses and clowns and counts 44 heads and 132 legs in his sleigh. Given that horses have one head and four legs, and clowns have one head and two legs, calculate the difference between the number of horses and clowns.

A. 0
B. 5
C. 22
D. 28
E. 132
F. More information is needed.

To start with, let C= Clowns and H= Horses.
For Heads: $C + H = 44$; For Legs: $2C + 4H = 132$
This now sets up your two equations that you can solve simultaneously.
$C = 44 - H$ so $2(44 - H) + 4H = 132$
Thus, $88 - 2H + 4H = 132$;
Therefore, $2H = 44; H = 22$
Substitute back in to give $C = 44 - H = 44 - 22 = 22$
Thus the difference between horses and clowns $= C - H = 22 - 22 = 0$

It's important you are able to do these types of questions quickly (and **without resorting to trial & error** as they are commonplace in section 1.

Diagrams

When a question asks about timetables, orders or sequences, draw out diagrams. By doing this, you can organise your thoughts and help make sense of the question.

"Mordor is West of Gondor but East of Rivendale. Lorien is midway between Gondor and Mordor. Erebus is West of Mordor. Eden is not East of Gondor."

*Which of the following **cannot** be concluded?*

A. Lorien is East of Erebus and Mordor.
B. Mordor is West of Gondor and East of Erebus.
C. Rivendale is west of Lorien and Gondor.
D. Gondor is East of Mordor and East of Lorien

E.   Erebus is West of Mordor and West of Rivendale.

Whilst it is possible to solve this in your head, it becomes much more manageable if you draw a quick diagram and plot the positions of each town:

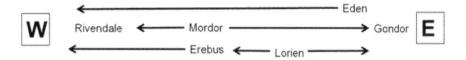

Now, it's a simple case of going through each option and seeing if it is correct according to the diagram. You can now easily see that Option E- Erebus cannot be west of Rivendale.

Don't feel that you have to restrict yourself to linear diagrams like this either – for some questions you may need to draw tables or even Venn diagrams. Consider the example:

Slifers and Osiris are not legendary. Krakens and Minotaurs are legendary. Minotaurs and Lords are both divine. Humans are neither legendary nor divine.

A.   Krakens may be only legendary or legendary and divine.
B.   Humans are not divine.
C.   Slifers are only divine.
D.   Osiris may be divine.
E.   Humans and Slifers are the same in terms of both qualities.

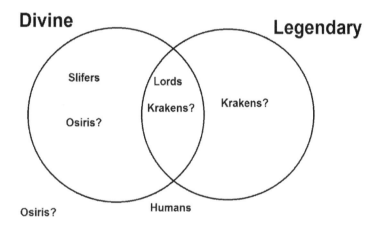

Constructing a Venn diagram allows us to quickly see that the position of Osiris and Krakens aren't certain. Thus, A and D must be true. Humans are neither so B is true. Krakens may be divine so A is true. E cannot be concluded as Slifers are divine but are humans are not. Thus, E is False.

Spatial Reasoning

There are usually 1-2 spatial reasoning questions every year. They usually give nets for a shape or a patterned cuboid and ask which options are possible rotations. Unfortunately, they are extremely difficult to prepare for because the skills necessary to solve these types of questions can take a very long time to improve. The best thing you can do to prepare is to familiarise yourself with the basics of how cube nets work and what the effect of transformations are e.g. what happens if a shape is reflected in a mirror etc.

It is also a good idea to try to learn to draw basic shapes like cubes from multiple angles if you can't do so already. Finally, remember that if the shape is straightforward like a cube, it might be easier for you to draw a net, cut it out and fold it yourself to see which of the options are possible.

Problem Solving Questions

Question 1:

The hospital coordinator is making the rota for the ward for next week; two of Drs Evans, James and Luca must be working on weekdays, none of them on Sundays and all of them on Saturdays. Dr Evans works 4 days a week including Mondays and Fridays. Dr Luca cannot work Monday or Thursday. Only Dr James can work 4 days consecutively, but he cannot do 5.

What days does Dr James work?

A. Saturday, Sunday and Monday.
B. Monday, Tuesday, Wednesday, Thursday and Saturday.
C. Monday, Thursday Friday and Saturday.
D. Tuesday, Wednesday, Friday and Saturday.
E. Monday, Tuesday, Wednesday, Thursday and Friday.

Question 2:

Michael, a taxi driver, charges a call out rate and a rate per mile for taxi rides. For a 4 mile ride he charges £11, and for a 5 mile ride, £13.

How much does he charge for a 9-mile ride?

A. £15   B. £17   C. £19   D. £20   E. £21

Question 3:

Goblins and trolls are not magical. Fairies and goblins are both mythical. Elves and fairies are magical. Gnomes are neither mythical nor magical.

Which of the following is **FALSE**?

A. Elves may be only magical or magical and mythical.
B. Gnomes are not mythical.
C. Goblins are only mythical.
D. Trolls may be mythical.
E. Gnomes and goblins are the same in terms of both qualities.

Question 4:

Jessica runs a small business making bespoke wall tiles. She has just had a rush order for 100 tiles placed that must be ready for today at 7pm. The client wants the tiles packed all together, a process which will take 15 minutes. Only 50 tiles can go in the kiln at any point and they must be put in the kiln to heat for 45 minutes. The tiles then sit in the kiln to cool before they can be packed, a process which takes 20 minutes. While tiles are in the kiln Jessica is able to decorate more tiles at a rate of 1 tile per minute.

What is the latest time Jessica can start making the tiles?

A. 2:55pm   B. 3:15pm   C. 3:30pm   D. 3:45pm

Question 5:

Pain nerve impulses are twice as fast as normal touch impulses. If Yun touches a boiling hot pan this message reaches her brain, 1 metre away, in 1 millisecond.

What is the speed of a normal touch impulse?

A. 5 m/s   B. 20 m/s   C. 50 m/s   D. 200m/s   E. 500 m/s

Question 6:

A woman has two children Melissa and Jack, yearly, their birthdays are 3 months apart, both being on the 22nd. The woman wishes to continue the trend of her children's names beginning with the same letter as the month they were born. If her next child, Alina is born on the 22nd 2 months after Jack's birthday, how many months after Alina is born will Melissa have her next birthday?

A. 2 months   B. 4 months   C. 5 months   D. 6 months   E. 7 months

Question 7:

Policemen work in pairs. PC Carter, PC Dirk, PC Adams and PC Bryan must work together but not for more than seven days in a row, which PC Adams and PC Bryan now have. PC Dirk has worked with PC Carter for 3 days in a row. PC Carter does not want to work with PC Adams if it can be avoided.

Who should work with PC Bryan?
A. PC Carter
B. PC Dirk
C. PC Adams
D. Nobody is available under the guidelines above.

Question 8:

My hair-dressers charges £30 for a haircut, £50 for a cut and blow-dry, and £60 for a full hair dye. They also do manicures, of which the first costs £15, and includes a bottle of nail polish, but are subsequently reduced by £5 if I bring my bottle of polish. The price is reduced by 10% if I book and pay for the next 5 appointments in advance and by 15% if I book at least the next 10.

I want to pay for my next 5 cut and blow-dry appointments, as well as for my next 3 manicures. How much will it cost?

A. £170   B. £255   C. £260   D. £285   E. £305

Question 9:

Alex, Bertha, David, Gemma, Charlie, Elena and Frankie are all members of the same family consisting of three children, two of whom, Frankie and Gemma are girls. No other assumption of gender based on name can be established. There are also four adults. Alex is a doctor and is David's brother. One of them is married to Elena, and they have two children. Bertha is married to David; Gemma is their child.
Who is Charlie?

A. Alex's daughter
B. Frankie's father
C. Gemma's brother
D. Elena's son
E. Gemma's sister

Question 10:

At 14:30 three medical students were asked to examine a patient's heart. Having already watched their colleague, the second two students were twice as fast as the first to examine. During the 8 minutes break after the final student had finished, they were told by their consultant that they had taken too long and so should go back and do the examinations again. The second time all the students took half as long as they had taken the first time with the exception of the first student who, instead took the same time as his two colleagues' second attempt. Assuming there was a one minute change over time between each student and they were finished by 15:15, how long did the second student take to examine the first time?

A. 3 minutes   B. 4 minutes   C. 6 minutes   D. 7 minutes   E. 8 minutes

Question 11:

I pay for 2 chocolate bars that cost £1.65 each with a £5 note. I receive 8 coins change, only 3 of which are the same.

Which **TWO** coins do I not receive in my change?

A. 1p   C. 5p   E. 20p   G. £1
B. 2p   D. 10p   F. £2

Question 12:

Two 140m long trains are running at the same speed in opposite directions. If they cross each other in 14 seconds then what is speed of each train?

A. 10 km/hr   B. 18 km/hr   C. 32 km/hr   D. 36 km/hr   E. 42 km/hr

Question 13:

Anil has to refill his home's swimming pool. He has four hoses which all run at different speeds. Alone, the first would completely fill the pool with water in 6 hours, the second in two days, the third in three days and the fourth in four days.

Using all the hoses together, how long will it take to fill the pool to the nearest quarter of an hour?

A. 4 hours 15 minutes
B. 4 hours 30 minutes
C. 4 hours 45 minutes
D. 5 hours
E. 5 hours 15 minutes

Question 14:

An ant is stuck in a 30 cm deep ditch. When the ant reaches the top of the ditch he will be able to climb out straight away. The ant is able to climb 3 cm upwards during the day, but falls back 2 cm at night.

How many days does it take for the ant to climb out of the ditch?

A. 27   B. 28   C. 29   D. 30   E. 31

Question 15:

When buying his ingredients a chef gets a discount of 10% when he buys 10 or more of each item, and 20% discount when he buys 20 or more. On one order he bought 5 sausages and 10 Oranges and paid £8.50. On another, he bought 10 sausages and 10 apples and paid £9, on a third he bought 30 oranges and paid £12.

How much would an order of 2 oranges, 13 sausages and 12 apples cost?

A. £12.52   B. £12.76   C. £13.52   D. £13.76   E. £13.80

Question 16:

My hairdressers encourage all of its clients to become members. By paying an annual member fee, the cost of haircuts decreases. VIP membership costs £125 annually with a £10 reduction on haircuts. Executive VIP membership costs £200 for the year with a £15 reduction per haircut. At the moment I am not a member and pay £60 per haircut. I know how many haircuts I have a year, and I work out that by becoming a member on either programme it would work out cheaper, and I would save the same amount of money per year on either programme.

How much will I save this year by buying membership?

A. £10   B. £15   C. £25   D. £30   E. £50

Question 17:

If criminals, thieves and judges are represented below:

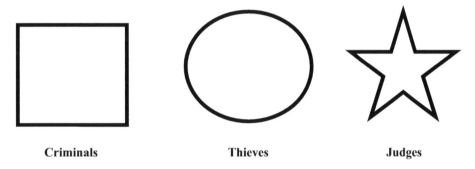

      Criminals   **Thieves**   **Judges**

Assuming that judges must have clean record, all thieves are criminals and all those who are guilty are convicted of their crimes, which of one of the following best represents their interaction?

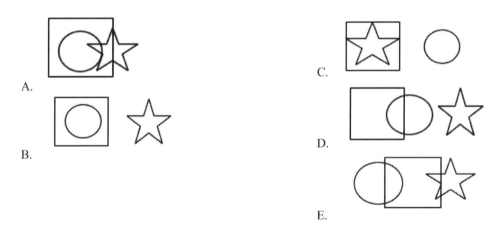

A.

B.

C.

D.

E.

Question 18:

The months of the year have been made into number codes. The code is comprised of three factors, including two of these being related the letters that make up the name of the month. No two months would have the same first number. But some such as March, which has the code 3513, have the same last number as others, such as May, which has the code 5313. October would be coded as 10715 while February is 286.

What would be the code for April?

A. 154   B. 441   C. 451   D. 514   E. 541

Question 19:

A mother gives yearly birthday presents of money to her children based on the age and their exam results. She gives them £5 each plus £3 for every year they are older than 5, and a further £10 for every A* they achieved in their results. Josie is 16 and gained 9 A*s in her results. Although Josie's brother Carson is 2 years older he receives £44 less a year for his birthday.

How many more A*s did Josie get than Carson?

A. 2   B. 3   C. 4   D. 5   E. 10

Question 20:

Apples are more expensive than pears, which are more expensive than oranges. Peaches are more expensive than oranges. Apples are less expensive than grapes.

Which two of the following must be true?

A. Grapes are less expensive than oranges.
B. Peaches may be less expensive than pears.
C. Grapes are more expensive than pears.
D. Pears and peaches are the same price.
E. Apples and peaches are the same price.

Question 21:

What is the minimum number of straight cutting motions needed to slice a cylindrical cake into 8 equally sized pieces?

A. 2   B. 3   C. 4   D. 5   E. 6   F. 8

Question 22:

Three friends, Mark, Russell and Tom had agreed to meet for lunch at 12 PM on Sunday. Daylight saving time (GMT+1) had started at 2 AM the same day, where clocks should be put forward by one hour. Mark's phone automatically changes the time but he does not realise this so when he wakes up he puts his phone forward an hour and uses his phone to time his arrival to lunch. Tom puts all of his clocks forward one hour at 7 AM. Russell forgets that the clocks should go forward, wakes at 10 AM doesn't change his clocks. All of the friends arrive on time as far as they are concerned.

Assuming that none of the friends realise any errors before arriving, which **TWO** of the following statements are **FALSE**?

A. Tom arrives at 12 PM (GMT +1).
B. All three friends arrive at the same time.
C. There is a 2 hour difference between when the first and last friend arrive.
D. Mark arrives late.
E. Mark arrives at 1 PM (GMT+3).
F. Russell arrives at 12 PM (GMT+0).

Question 23:

A class of young students has a pet spider. Deciding to play a practical joke on their teacher, one day during morning break one of the students put the spider in their teachers' desk. When first questioned by the head teacher, Mr Jones, the five students who were in the classroom during morning break all lied about what they saw. Realising that the students were all lying, Mr Jones called all 5 students back individually and, threatened with suspension, all the students told the truth. Unfortunately Mr Jones only wrote down the student's statements not whether they had been told in the truthful or lying questioning.

The students' two statements appear below:

Archie: "It wasn't Edward. "

     "It was Bella."   **Charlotte**: "It was Edward."

                                        "It wasn't Archie"

Darcy: "It was Charlotte"

     "It was Bella"   **Bella**: "It wasn't Charlotte."

                                       "It wasn't Edward."

Edward: "It was Darcy"

     "It wasn't Archie"

Who put the spider in the teacher's desk?

A.   Edward   D.   Charlotte

B.   Bella   E.   More information needed.

C.   Darcy

Question 24:

Dr Massey wants to measure out 0.1 litres of solution. Unfortunately the lab assistant dropped the 200 ml measuring cylinder, and so the scientist only has a 300 ml and a half litre-measuring beaker. Assuming he cannot accurately use the beakers to measure anything less than their full capacity, what is the minimum volume he will have to use to be able to ensure he measures the right amount?

A.   100 ml   C.   300 ml   E.   500 ml

B.   200 ml   D.   400 ml   F.   600 ml

Question 25:

Francis lives on a street with houses all consecutively numbered evenly. When one adds up the value of all the house numbers it totals 870.

In order to determine Francis' house number:

1.   The relative position of Francis' house must be known.

2.   The number of houses in the street must be known.

3.   At least three of the house numbers must be known.

A.   1 only   D.   1 and 2

B.   2 only   E.   2 and 3

C.   3 only

Question 26:

There were 20 people exercising in the cardio room of a gym. Four people were about to leave when suddenly a man collapsed on one of the machines. Fortunately a doctor was on the machine beside him. Emerging from his office, one of the personal trainers called an ambulance. In the 5 minutes that followed before the two paramedics arrived, half of the people who were leaving, left upon hearing the commotion, and eight people came in from the changing rooms to hear the paramedics pronouncing the man dead.

How many living people were left in the room?

A. 25   B. 26   C. 27   D. 28   E. 29   F. 30

Question 27:

A man and woman are in an accident. They both suffer the same trauma, which causes both of them to lose blood at a rate of 0.2 Litres/minute. At normal blood volume the man has 8 litres and the woman 7 litres, and people collapse when they lose 40% of their normal blood volume.

Which **TWO** of the following are true?

A.   The man will collapse 2 minutes before the woman.
B.   The woman collapses 2 minutes before the man.
C.   The total blood loss is 5 litres.
D.   The woman has 4.2 litres of blood in her body when she collapses.
E.   The man's blood loss is 4.8 litres when he collapses.
F.   Blood loss is at a rate of 2 litres every 12 minutes.

Question 28:

Jenny, Helen and Rachel have to run a distance of 13 km. Jenny runs at a pace of 8 kmph, Helen at a pace of 10 kmph, and Rachel 11 kmph.

If Jenny sets off 15 minutes before Helen, and 25 minutes before Rachel, what order will they arrive at the destination?

A.   Jenny, Helen, Rachel.   D.   Rachel, Helen, Jenny.
B.   Helen, Rachel, Jenny.   E.   Jenny, Rachel, Helen.
C.   Helen, Jenny, Rachel.   F.   None of the above.

Question 29:

On a specific day at a GP surgery 150 people visited the surgery and common complaints were recorded as a percentage of total patients. Each patient could use their appointment to discuss up to 2 complaints. 56% flu-like symptoms, 48% pain, 20% diabetes, 40% asthma or COPD, 30% high blood pressure.

Which statement **must** be true?
A.   A minimum of 8 patients complained of pain and flu-like symptoms.
B.   No more than 45 patients complained of high blood pressure and diabetes.
C.   There were a minimum of 21 patients who did not complain about flu-like symptoms or high blood pressure.
D.   There were actually 291 patients who visited the surgery.
E.   None of the above.

Question 30:

All products in a store were marked up by 15%. They were subsequently reduced in a sale with quoted saving of 25% from the higher price. What is the true reduction from the original price?
A.   5%   D.   18.25%
B.   10%   E.   20%
C.   13.75%   F.   None of the above.

Question 31:

A recipe states it makes 12 pancakes and requires the following ingredients: 2 eggs, 100g plain flour, and 300ml milk. Steve is cooking pancakes for 15 people and wants to have sufficient mixture for 3 pancakes each.

What quantities should Steve use to ensure this whilst using whole eggs?
A. 2½ eggs, 125g plain flour, 375ml milk
B. 3 eggs , 150g plain flour, 450 ml milk
C. 7½ eggs, 375g plain flour, 1125 ml milk
D. 8 eggs, 400g plain flour, 1200 ml milk
E. 12 eggs, 600g plain flour, 1800 ml milk
F. None of the above.

Question 32:

Spring Cleaning cleaners buy industrial bleach from a warehouse and dilute it twice before using it domestically. The first dilution is by 9:1 and then the second, 4:1.

If the cleaners require 6 litres of diluted bleach, how much warehouse bleach do they require?
A. 30 ml
B. 120 ml
C. 166 ml
D. 666 ml
E. 1,200 ml
F. None of the above

Question 33:

During a GP consultation in 2015, Ms Smith tells the GP about her grandchildren. Ms Smith states that Charles is the middle grandchild and was born in 2002. In 2010, Bertie was twice the age of Adam and that in 2015 there are 5 years between Bertie and Adam. Charles and Adam are separated by 3 years.

How old are the 3 grandchildren in 2015?
A. Adam = 16, Bertie = 11, Charles = 13
B. Adam = 5, Bertie = 10, Charles = 8
C. Adam = 10, Bertie = 15, Charles = 13
D. Adam = 10, Bertie = 20, Charles = 13
E. Adam = 11, Bertie = 10, Charles = 8
F. More information needed.

Question 34:

Kayak Hire charges a fixed flat rate and then an additional half-hourly rate. Peter hires the kayak for 3 hours and pays £14.50, and his friend Kevin hires 2 kayaks for 4hrs30mins each and pays £41. How much would

Tom pay to hire one kayak for 2 hours?
A. £8
B. £10.50
C. £15
D. £33.20
E. £35.70
F. None of the above.

Question 35:

A ticketing system uses a common digital display of numbers 0 – 9. The number 7 is showing. However, a number of the light elements are not currently working.

Which set of the following digits is possible?
A. 3, 4, 7
B. 0, 1, 9
C. 2, 7, 8
D. 0, 5, 9
E. 3, 8, 9
F. 3, 4, 9

Question 36:

A team of 4 builders take 12 days of 7 hours work to complete a house. The company decides to recruit 3 extra builders.

How many 8 hour days will it take the new workforce to build a house?

A. 2 days
B. 6 days
C. 7 days
D. 10 days
E. 12 days
F. More information needed

Question 37:

All astragalus are fabacaea as are all gummifer. Acacia are not astragalus. Which of the following statements is true?

A. Acacia are not fabacaea.
B. No astragalus are also gummifer.
C. All fabacae are astragalus or gummifer.
D. Some acacia may be fabacaea.
E. Gummifer are all acacia.
F. None of the above.

Question 38:

The Smiths want to reupholster both sides of their seating cushions (dimensions shown on diagram). The fabric they are using costs £10/m, can only be bought in whole metre lengths and has a standard width of 1m. Each side of a cushion must be made from a single peice of fabric. The seamstress changes a flat rate of £25 per cushion. How much will it cost them to reupholster 4 cushions?

A. £ 20
B. £ 80
C. £ 110
D. £ 130
E. £ 150
F. £ 200

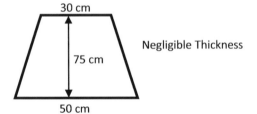

Question 39:

Lisa buys a cappuccino from either Milk or Beans Coffee shops each day. The quality of the coffee is the same but she wishes to work out the relative costs once the loyalty scheme has been taken into account. In Milk, a regular cappuccino is £2.40, and in Beans, £2.15. However, the loyalty scheme in Milk gives Lisa a free cappuccino for every 9 she buys, whereas Beans use a points system of 10 points per full pound spent (each point is worth 1p) which can be used to cover the cost of a full cappuccino.

If Lisa buys a cappuccino each day of September, which coffee shop would work out cheaper, and by how much?

A. Milk, by £4.60
B. Beans by £6.30
C. Beans, by £4.60
D. Beans, by £2.45
E. Milk, by £2.45
F. Milk, by £6.25

Question 40:

Paula needs to be at a meeting in Notting Hill at 11am. The route requires her to walk 5 minutes to the 283 bus which takes 25 minutes, and then change to the 220 bus which takes 14 minutes. Finally she walks for 3 minutes to her meeting. If the 283 bus comes every 10 minutes, and the 220 bus at 0 minutes, 20 minutes and 40 minutes past the hour, what is the latest time she can leave and still be at her meeting on time?

A. 09.45   B. 09.58   C. 10.01   D. 10.05   E. 10.10   F. 10.15

Question 41:

Two trains, a high speed train A and a slower local train B, travel from Manchester to London. Train A travels the first 20 km at 100 km/hr and then at an average speed of 150km/hr. Train B travels at a constant average speed of 90 km/hr. If train B leaves 20 minutes before train A, at what distance will train A pass train B?

A. 75 km   B. 90 km   C. 100 km   D. 120 km   E. 150 km

Question 42:

The university gym has an upfront cost of £35 with no contract fee, but classes are charged at £3 each. The local gym has no joining fee and is £15 per month. What is the minimum number of classes I need to attend in a 12 month period to make the local gym cheaper than the university gym?

A. 40   B. 48   C. 49   D. 50   E. 55   F. 60

Question 43:

"All medicines are drugs, but not all drugs are medicines", goes a well-known saying. If we accept this statement as true, and consider that all antibiotics are medicines, but no herbal drugs are medicines, then which of the following is definitely **FALSE**?

A. Some herbal drugs are not medicines.   C. Some herbal drugs are antibiotics.
B. All antibiotics are drugs.   D. Some medicines are antibiotics

Question 44:

Sonia has been studying the paths taken by various trains travelling between London and Edinburgh on the East coast. Trains can stop at the following stations: Newark, Peterborough, Doncaster, York, Northallerton, Darlington, Durham and Newcastle.

She notes the following:

-    All trains stop at Peterborough, York, Darlington and Newcastle.
-    All trains which stop at Northallerton also stop at Durham.
-    Each day, 50% of the trains stop at both Newark *and* Northallerton.
-    All designated "Fast" trains make less than 5 stops. All other trains make 5 stops or more.
-    On average, 16 trains run each day.

Which of the following can be reliably concluded from these observations?
A. All trains, which are not designated "fast" trains, must stop at Durham.
B. No more than 8 trains on any 1 day will stop at Northallerton.
C. No designated "Fast" trains will stop at Durham.
D. It is possible for a train to make 5 stops, including Northallerton.
E. A train which stops at Newark will also stop at Durham.

Question 45:

Rakton is 5 miles directly north of Blueville. Gallford is 8 miles directly south of Haston. Lepstone is situated 5 miles directly east of Blueville, and 5 miles directly west of Gallford.

Which of the following **CANNOT** be reliably concluded from this information?
A. Lepstone is South of Rakton
B. Haston is North of Rakton
C. Gallford is East of Rakton
D. Blueville is East of Haston

E.   Haston is North of Lepstone

Question 46:

The Eastminster Parliament is undergoing a new set of elections. There are 600 seats up for election, each of which will be elected separately by the people living in that constituency. 6 parties win at least 1 seat in the election, the Blue Party, the Red party, the Orange party, the Yellow party, the Green party and the Purple party. In order to form a government, a party (or coalition) must hold *over* 50% of the seats. After the election, a political analysis committee produces the following report:

-   No party has gained more than 45% of the seats, so nobody is able to form a government by themselves.
-   The red and the blue party each gained over 40% of the seats.
-   No other party gained more than 4% of the seats.
-   The green party gained the 4th highest number of seats.

The red party work out that if they collaborate with the green party and the orange party, between the 3 of them, they will have enough seats to form a coalition government.

What is the minimum number of seats that the green party could have?

A. 5   C. 7   E. 9

B. 6   D. 8   F. 10

Questions 47-51 are based on the following information:

A grandmother wants to give her 5 grandchildren £100 between them for Christmas this year. She wants to grade the money she gives to each grandchild exactly so that the older children receive more than the younger ones. She wants share the money such that she will give the 2nd youngest child as much more than the youngest, as the 3rd youngest gets than the 2nd youngest, as the 4th youngest gets from the 3rd youngest and so on. The result will be that the two youngest children together will get seven times as less money than the three oldest.

M is the amount of money the youngest child receives, and D the difference between the amount the youngest and 2nd youngest children receive.

Question 47:

What is the expression for the amount the oldest child receives?

A. M C. $2M$ E. $M + 4D$

B. $M + D$ D. $4M^2$ F. None of the above.

Question 48:

What is the correct expression for the total money received?

A. $5M = £100$ D. $5M + 10D = £100$

B. $5D + 10M = £100$

C. $D = \dfrac{M}{100}$ E. $M = \dfrac{2D}{11}$

Question 49:

"The two youngest children together will get seven times less money than the three oldest."

Which one of the following best expresses the above statement?

A. $7(3M + 9D) = 2M + D$ C. $7(2M + D) = 3M + 9D$

B. $7D = M$ D. $2(7M + D) = 3M + 9D$

Question 50:

Using the statement in the previous question, what is the correct expression for M?

A. $\dfrac{2D}{11}$ B. $\dfrac{2}{11}$ C. $\dfrac{10D}{11}$ D. $\dfrac{120}{11}$

Question 51:

Express £100 in terms of D.

A. $£100 = \dfrac{120D}{11}$

B. $£100 = \dfrac{120D}{10}$

C. $£100 = \dfrac{120}{11D}$

D. $£100 = 21D$

E. $£100 = 5M + 10D$

Question 52:

Four young girls entered a local baking competition. Though a bit burnt, Ellen's carrot cake did not come last. The girl who baked a Madeira sponge had practiced a lot, and so came first, while Jaya came third with her entry. Aleena did better than the girl who made the Tiramisu, and the girl who made the Victoria sponge did better than Veronica.

Which **TWO** of the following were **NOT** results of the competition?

A. Veronica made a tiramisu
B. Ellen came second
C. Aleena made a Victoria sponge
D. The Victoria sponge came in 3rd place
E. The carrot cake came 3rd

Question 53:

In a young children's football league of 5 teams were; Celtic Changers, Eire Lions, Nordic Nesters, Sorten Swipers and the Whistling Winners. One of the boys playing in the league, after being asked by his parents, said that while he could remember the other teams' total points he could not remember his own, the Eire Lions, score. He said that all the teams played each other and when teams lost they were given 0 points, when they drew, 1 point, and 3 for a win. He remembered that the Celtic Changers had a total of 2 points; the Sorten Swipers had 5; the Nordic Nesters had 8, and the Whistling Winners 1.

How many did the boy's team score?

A. 1   C. 8   E. 11
B. 4   D. 10   F. None of the above.

Question 54:

T is the son of Z, Z and J are sisters, R is the mother of J and S is the son of R.

Which one of the following statements is correct?

A. T and J are cousins
B. S and J are sisters
C. J is the maternal uncle of T
D. S is the maternal uncle of T
E. R is the grandmother of Z.

Question 55:

John likes to shoot bottles off a shelf. In the first round he places 16 bottles on the shelf and knocks off 8 bottles. 3 of the knocked off bottles are damaged and can no longer be used, whilst 1 bottle is lost. He puts the undamaged bottles back on the shelf before continuing. In the second round he shoots six times and misses 50% of these shots. He damages two bottles with every shot which does not miss. 2 bottles also fall off the shelf at the end. He puts up 2 new bottles before continuing. In the final round, John misses all his shots and in frustration, knocks over gets angry and knocks over 50% of the remaining bottles.

How many bottles were left on the wall after the final round?

A. 2   C. 4   E. 6
B. 3   D. 5   F. More information needed.

Questions 56 - 62 are based on the information below:

All lines are named after a station they serve, apart from the Oval and Rectangle lines, which are named for their recognisable shapes. Trains run in both directions.

➤ There are express trains that run from end to end of the St Mark's and Straightly lines in 5 and 6 minutes respectively.

➤ It takes 2 minutes to change between St Mark's and both Oval and Rectangle lines, 1 minute between Rectangle and Oval.

➤ It takes 3 minutes to change between the Straightly and all other lines, except with the St Mark's line which only takes 30 seconds

➤ The Straightly line is a fast line and takes only 2 minutes between stops apart from to and from Keyton, which only takes 1 minute, and to and from Lime St which takes 3 minutes.

➤ The Oval line is much slower and takes 4 minutes between stops, apart from between Baxton and Marven, and also Archite and West Quays, which takes 5 minutes.

➤ The Rectangle line a reliable line; never running late but as a consequence is much slower taking 6 minutes between stops.

➤ The St Mark's line is fast and takes 2 and half minutes between stations.

➤ If a passenger reaches the end of the line, it takes three minutes to change onto a train travelling back in the opposite direction.

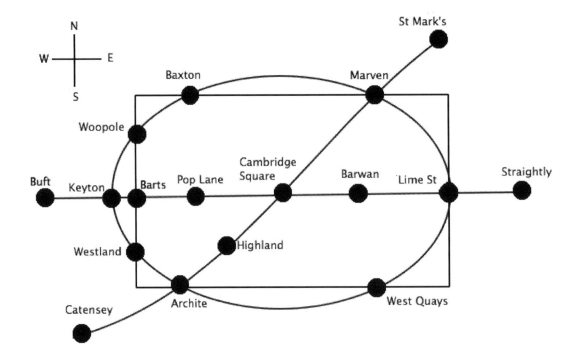

Question 56:

Assuming all lines are running on time, how long does it take to go from St Mark's to Archite on the St Mark's line?

A. 5 minutes
B. 6 minutes
C. 7.5 minutes

D. 10 minutes
E. 12.5 minutes

Question 57:

Assuming all lines are running on time, what's the shortest time it will take to go from Buft to Straightly?

A. 6 minutes
B. 10 minutes
C. 12 minutes

D. 14 minutes
E. 16 minutes

Question 58:

What is the shortest time it will take to go from Baxton to Pop Lane?

A. 11 minutes
B. 12 minutes
C. 13 minutes

D. 14 minutes
E. 15 minutes

Question 59:

Which station, even at the quickest journey time, is furthest in terms of time from Cambridge Square?

A. Catensey   B. Buft   C. Woopole   D. Westland

Questions 60-62 use this additional information:

On a difficult day there are signal problems whereby all lines except the reliable line are delayed, such that train travel times between stations are doubled. These delays have caused overcrowding at the platforms which means that while changeover times between lines are still the same, passengers always have to wait an extra 5 minutes on all of the platforms before catching the next train.

Question 60:

At best, how long will it now take to go from Westland to Marven?

A. 25 minutes
B. 29 minutes
C. 30 minutes

D. 33 minutes
E. 35 minutes

Question 61:

There is a bus that goes from Baxton to Archite and takes 27-31 minutes. Susan lives in Baxton and needs to get to her office in Archite as quickly as possible. With all the delays and lines out of service,

How should you advise Susan best to get to work?

A. Baxton to Archite via Barts using the Rectangle line.
B. Baxton to Woopole on the Rectangle line, then Oval to Archite via Keyton.
C. It is not possible to tell between the fastest two options.
D. Baxton to Woopole on the Rectangle line, then Oval to Archite via Keyton.
E. Baxton to Archite on the Oval line.
F. Baxton to Archite using the bus.

Question 62:

In addition to the delays the Oval line signals fail completely, so the line falls out of service. How long will it now take to go from St Mark's to West Quays as quickly as possible?

A. 35 minutes
B. 30 minutes

C. 33 minutes
D. 29 minutes

E. 30.5 minutes
F. None of the above.

Question 63:

In an unusual horserace, only 4 horses, each with different racing colours and numbers competed. Simon's horse wore number 1. Lila's horse wasn't painted yellow nor blue, and the horse that wore 3, which was wearing red, beat the horse that came in third. Only one horse wore the same number as the position it finished in. Arthur's horse beat Simon's horse, whereas Celia's horse beat the horse that wore number 1. The horse wearing green, Celia's, came second, and the horse wearing blue wore number 4. Which one of the following must be true?

A. Simon's horse was yellow and placed 3rd.
B. Celia's horse was red.
C. Celia's horse was in third place.
D. Arthur's horse was blue.
E. Lila's horse wore number 4.

Question 64:

Jessie plants a tree with a height of 40 cm. The information leaflet states that the plant should grow by 20% each year for the first 2 years, and then 10% each year thereafter.

What is the expected height at 4 years?
A. 58.08 cm
B. 64.89 cm
C. 69.696 cm
D. 89.696 cm
E. 82.944 cm
F. None of the above

Question 65:

A company is required to pay each employee 10% of their wage into a pension fund if their annual total wage bill is above £200,000. However, there is a legal loophole that if the company splits over two sites, the £200,000 bill is per site. The company therefore decides to have an east site, and a west site.

Name	Annual Salary (£)
Luke	47,000
John	78,400
Emma	68,250
Nicola	88,500
Victoria	52,500
Daniel	63,000

Which employees should be grouped at the same site to minimise the cost to the company?

A. John, Nicola, Luke
B. Nicola, Victoria, Daniel
C. Nicola, Daniel, Luke
D. John, Daniel, Emma
E. Luke, Victoria, Emma

Question 66:

A bus takes 24 minutes to travel from White City to Hammersmith with no stops. Each time the bus stops to pick up and/or drop off passengers, it takes approximately 90 seconds. This morning, the bus picked up passengers from 5 stops, and dropped off passengers at 7 stops.

What is the minimum journey time from White City to Hammersmith this morning?
A. 28 minutes
B. 34 minutes
C. 34.5 minutes
D. 36 minutes
E. 37.5 minutes
F. 42 minutes

Question 67:

Sally is making a Sunday roast for her family and is planning her schedule regarding cooking times. The chicken takes 15 minutes to prepare, 75 minutes to cook, and needs to stand for exactly 5 minutes after cooking. The potatoes take 18 minutes to prepare, 5 minutes to boil, then 50 minutes to roast, and must be roasted immediately after boiling, and then served immediately. The vegetables require only 5 minutes preparation time and 8 minutes boiling time before serving, and can be kept warm to be served at any time after cooking. Given that the cooker can only be cooking two items at any given time and Sally can prepare only one item at a time, what should Sally's schedule be if she wishes to serve dinner at 4pm and wants to start cooking each item as late as possible?

A. Chicken 2.25, potatoes 2.47, vegetables 2.42

B. Chicken 2.25, potatoes 2.47, vegetables 3.47

C. Chicken 2.35, potatoes 3.47, vegetables 2.47

D. Chicken 2.35, potatoes 2.47, vegetables 3.47

E. Chicken 2.45, potatoes 3.47, vegetables 2.47

F. Chicken 2.45, potatoes 2.47, vegetables 3.47

Question 68:

The Smiths have 4 children whose total age is 80. Paul is double the age of Jeremy. Annie is exactly half way between the ages of Jeremy and Paul, and Rebecca is 2 years older than Paul. How old are each of the children?

A. Paul 23, Jeremy 12, Rebecca 26, Annie 19.

B. Paul 22, Jeremy, 11, Rebecca 24, Annie 16.

C. Paul 24, Jeremy 12, Rebecca 26, Annie 18.

D. Paul 28, Jeremy 14, Rebecca 30, Annie 21.

E. More information needed.

Question 69:

Sarah has a jar of spare buttons that are a mix of colours and sizes. The jar contains the following assortment of buttons:

	10mm	25mm	40mm
Cream	15	22	13
Red	6	15	7
Green	9	19	8
Blue	20	6	15
Yellow	4	8	26
Black	17	16	14
Total	**71**	**86**	**83**

Sarah wants to use a 25mm diameter button, but doesn't mind if it is cream or yellow. What is the maximum number of buttons she will have to remove in order to guarantee to pick a suitable button on the next attempt?

A. 210

B. 218

C. 219

D. 239

E. None of the above

Question 70:

Ben wants to optimise his score with one throw of a dart. 50% of the time he hits a segment to either side of the one he is aiming at. With this in mind, which segment should he aim for?

[Ignore all double/triple modifiers]

A. 15

B. 16

C. 17

D. 18

E. 19

F. 20

Question 71:

Victoria is completing her weekly shop, and the total cost of the items is £8.65. She looks in her purse and sees that she has a £5 note, and a large amount of change, including all types of coins. She uses the £5 note, and pays the remainder using the maximum number of coins possible in order to remove some weight from the purse. However, the store has certain rules she has to follow when paying:

- No more than 20p can be paid in "bronze" change (the name given to any combination of 1p pieces and 2p pieces)
- No more than 50p can be paid using any combination of 5p pieces and 10p pieces.
- No more than £1.50 can be paid using any combination of 20p pieces and 50p pieces.

Victoria pays the exact amount, and does not receive any change. Under these rules, what is the *maximum* number of coins that Victoria can have paid with?

A. 30   B. 31   C. 36   D. 41   E. 46

Question 72:

I look at the clock on my bedside table, and I see the following digits:

However, I also see that there is a glass of water between me and the clock, which is in front of 2 adjacent figures. I know that this means these 2 figures will appear reversed. For example, 10 would appear as 01, and 20 would appear as 05 (as 5 on a digital clock is a reversed image of a 2). Some numbers, such as 3, cannot appear reversed because there are no numbers which look like the reverse of 3.

Which of the following could be the actual time?

A. 15:52   B. 21:25   C. 12:55   D. 12:22   E. 21:52

Question 73:

Slavica has invaded Worsid, whilst Nordic has invaded Lorkdon. Worsid, spotting an opportunity to bolster its amount of land and natural resources, invades Nordic. Each of these countries is either a dictatorship or a democracy. Slavica is a dictatorship, but Lorkdon is a democracy. 10 years ago, a treaty was signed which guaranteed that no democracy would invade another democracy. No dictatorship has both invaded another dictatorship *and* been invaded by another dictatorship.

Assuming the aforementioned treaty has been upheld, what style of government is practiced in Worsid?

A. Worsid is a Dictatorship.

B. Worsid is a Democracy.

C. Worsid does not practice either of these forms of government.

D. It is impossible to tell.

Question 74:

Sheila is on a shift at the local supermarket. Unfortunately, the till has developed a fault, meaning it cannot tell her how much change to give each customer. A customer is purchasing the following items, at the following costs:

- A packet of grated cheese priced at £3.25
- A whole cucumber, priced at 75p
- A fish pie mix, priced at £4.00
- 3 DVDs, each priced at £3.00

Sheila knows there is an offer on DVDs in the store at present, in which 3 DVDs bought together will only cost £8.00. The customer pays with a £50 note.

How much change will Sheila need to give the customer?

A. £4   B. £33   C. £34   D. £36   E. £38

Question 75:

Ryan is cooking breakfast for several guests at his hotel. He is frying most of the items using the same large frying pan, to get as much food prepared in as little time as possible. Ryan is cooking Bacon, Sausages, and eggs in this pan. He calculates how much room is taken up in the pan by each item. He calculates the following:

- Each rasher of bacon takes up 7% of the available space in the pan
- Each sausage takes up 3% of the available space in the pan.
- Each egg takes up 12% of the available space in the pan.

Ryan is cooking 2 rashers of bacon, 4 sausages and 1 egg for each guest. He decides to cook all the food for each guest at the same time, rather than cooking all of each item at once.

How many guests can he cook for at once?

A. 1   B. 2   C. 3   D. 4   E. 5

Question 76:

SafeEat Inc. is a national food development testing agency. The Manchester-based laboratory has a system for recording all the laboratory employees' birthdays, and presenting them with cake on their birthday, in order to keep staff morale high. Certain amounts of petty cash are set aside each month in order to fund this. 40% of the staff have their birthday in March, and the secretary works out that £60 is required to fund the birthday cake scheme during this month.

If all birthdays cost £2 to provide a cake for, how many people work at the laboratory?

A. 45   B. 60   C. 75   D. 100   E. 150

Question 77:

Many diseases, such as cancer, require specialist treatment, and thus cannot be treated by a general practitioner. Instead, these diseases must be *referred* to a specialist after an initial, more generalised, medical assessment. Bob has had a biopsy on the 1st of August on a lump found in his abdomen. The results show that it is a tumour, with a slight chance of becoming metastatic, so he is referred to a waiting list for specialist radiotherapy and chemotherapy. The average waiting time in the UK for such treatment is 3 weeks, but in Bob's local district, high demand means that it takes 50% longer for each patient to receive treatment. As he is a lower risk case, with a low risk of metastasis, his waiting time is extended by another 20%.

How many weeks will it be before Bob receives specialist treatment?

A. 4.5   B. 4.6   C. 5.0   D. 5.1   E. 5.4   F. 5.6

Question 78:

In a class of 30 seventeen year old students, 40% drink alcohol at least once a month. Of those who drink alcohol at least once a month, 75% drink alcohol at least once a week. 1 in 3 of the students who drink alcohol at least once a week also smoke marijuana. 1 in 3 of the students who drink alcohol less than once a month also smoke marijuana.

How many of the students in total smoke marijuana?

A. 3   B. 4   C. 6   D. 9   E. 10   F. 15

Question 79:

Complete the following sequence of numbers: 1, 4, 10, 22, 46, …

A. 84   B. 92   C. 94   D. 96   E. 100

Question 80:

If the mean of 5 numbers is 7, the median is 8 and the mode is 3, what must the two largest numbers in the set of numbers add up to?

A. 14   C. 24   E. 35
B. 21   D. 26   F. More information needed.

Question 81:

Ahmed buys 1kg bags of potatoes from the supermarket. 1kg bags have to weigh between 900 and 1100 grams. In the first week, there are 10 potatoes in the bag. The next week, there are only 5. Assuming that the potatoes in the bag in week 1 are all the same weight as each other, and the potatoes in the bag in week 2 are all the same weight as each other, what is the maximum possible difference between the heaviest and lightest potato in the two bags?

A. 50g   B. 70g   C. 90g   D. 110g   E. 130g

Question 82:

A football tournament involves a group stage, then a knockout stage. In the group stage, groups of four teams play in a round robin format (i.e. each team plays every other team once) and the team that wins the most matches in each group proceeds through to a knockout stage. In addition, the single best performing second place team across all the groups gains a place in the knockout stage. In the knockout stage, sets of two teams play each other and the one that wins proceeds to the next round until there are two teams left, who play the final.

If we start with 60 teams, how many matches are played altogether?

A. 75   B. 90   C. 100   D. 105   E. 165

Question 83:

The last 4 digits of my card number are 2 times my PIN number, plus 200. The last 4 digits of my husband's card number are the last four digits of my card number doubled, plus 200. My husband's PIN number is 2 times the last 4 digits of his card number, plus 200. Given that all these numbers are 4 digits long, whole numbers, and cannot begin with 0, what is the largest number my PIN number can be?

A. 1,074   C. 2,348   E. 9,999
B. 1,174   D. 4,096   F. More information needed.

Question 84:

All women between 50 and 70 in the UK are invited for breast cancer screening every 3 years. Patients at Doddinghurst Surgery are invited for screening for the first time at any point between their 50th and 53rd birthday. If they ignore an invitation, they are sent reminders every 5 months. We can assume that a woman is screened exactly 1 month after she is sent the invitation or reminder that she accepts. The next invitation for screening is sent exactly 3 years after the previous screening.

If a woman accepts the screening on the second reminder each time, what is the youngest she can be when she has her 4th screening?

A. 60   B. 61   C. 62   D. 63   E. 64   F. 65

Question 85:

Ellie gets a pay rise of k thousand pounds on every anniversary of joining the company, where k is the number of years she has been at the company. She currently earns £40,000, and she has been at the company for 5.5 years. What was her salary when she started at the company?

A. £25,000   C. £28,000   E. £31,000
B. £27,000   D. £30,000   F. £32,000

Question 86:

Northern Line trains arrive into Kings Cross station every 8 minutes, Piccadilly Line trains every 5 minutes and Victoria Line trains every 2 minutes. If trains from all 3 lines arrived into the station exactly 15 minutes ago, how long will it be before they do so again?

A. 24 minutes   C. 40 minutes   E. 65 minutes
B. 25 minutes   D. 60 minutes   F. 80 minutes

Question 87:

If you do not smoke or drink alcohol, your risk of getting Disease X is 1 in 12. If you smoke, you are half as likely to get Disease X as someone who does not smoke. If you drink alcohol, you are twice as likely to get Disease X. A new drug is released that halves anyone's total risk of getting Disease X for each tablet taken. How many tablets of the drug would someone who drinks alcohol have to take to reduce their risk to the same level as someone who smoked but did not take the drug?

A. 0   B. 1   C. 2   D. 3   E. 4   F. 5

Questions 88 – 90 refer to the following information:

There are 20 balls in a bag. 1/2 are red. 1/10 of those that are not red are yellow. The rest are green except 1, which is blue.

Question 88:

If I draw 2 balls from the bag (without replacement), what is the most likely combination to draw?

A. Red and green   C. Red and red
B. Red and yellow   D. Blue and yellow

Question 89:

If I draw 2 balls from the bag (without replacement), what is the least likely (without being impossible) combination to draw?

A. Blue and green   C. Yellow and yellow
B. Blue and yellow   D. Yellow and green

Question 90:

How many balls do you have to draw (without replacement) to guarantee getting at least one of at least three different colours?

A. 5   B. 12   C. 13   D. 17   E. 18   F. 19

Question 91:

A general election in the UK resulted in a hung parliament, with no single party gaining more than 50% of the seats. Thus, the main political parties are engaged in discussion over the formation of a coalition government. The results of this election are shown below:

Political Party	Seats won
Conservatives	260
Labour	270
Liberal Democrats	50
UKIP	35
Green Party	20
Scottish National Party	17
Plaid Cymru	13
Sinn Fein	9
Democratic Unionist Party (DUP)	11
Other	14 (14 other parties won 1 seat each)

There are a total of 699 seats, meaning that in order to form a government, any coalition must have at least 350 seats between them. Several of the party leaders have released statements about who they are and are not willing to form a coalition with, which are summarised as follows:

– The Conservative party and Labour are not willing to take part in a coalition together.
– The Liberal Democrats refuse to take part in any coalition which also involves UKIP.
– The Labour party will only form a coalition with UKIP if the Green party are also part of this coalition.
– The Conservative party are not willing to take part in any coalition with UKIP unless the Liberal Democrats are also involved.

Considering this information, what is the minimum number of parties required to form a coalition government?

A) 2   B) 3   C) 4   D) 5   E) 6

Question 92:

On Tuesday, 360 patients attend appointments at Doddinghurst Surgery. Of the appointments that are booked in, only 90% are attended. Of the appointments that are booked in, 1 in 2 are for male patients, the remaining appointments are for female patients. Male patients are three times as likely to miss their booked appointment as female patients.

How many male patients attend appointments at Doddinghurst Surgery on Tuesday?

A. 30   B. 60   C. 130   D. 150   E. 170

Question 93:

Every A Level student at Greentown Sixth Form studies Maths. Additionally, 60% study Biology, 50% study Economics and 50% study Chemistry. The other subject on offer at Greentown Sixth Form is Physics. Assuming every student studies 3 subjects and that there are 60 students altogether, how many students study Physics?

A. 15   C. 30   E. 60

B. 24   D. 40   F.   More information needed

Question 94:

100,000 people are diagnosed with chlamydia each year in the UK. An average of 0.6 sexual partners are informed per diagnosis. Of these, 80% have tests for chlamydia themselves. Half of these tests come back positive.

Assuming that each of the people diagnosed has had an average of 3 sexual partners (none of them share sexual partners or have sex with each other) and that the likelihood of having chlamydia is the same for those partners who are tested and those who are not, how many of the sexual partners who were not tested (whether they were informed or not) have chlamydia?

A. 120,000   C. 136,000   E. 240,000

B. 126,000   D. 150,000   F.   252,000

Question 95:

In how many different positions can you place an additional tile to make a straight line of 3 tiles?

A. 6
B. 7
C. 8
D. 9
E. 10
F. 11
G. 12

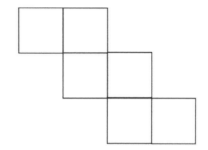

Question 96:

Harry is making orange squash for his daughter's birthday party. He wants to have a 200ml glass of squash for each of the 20 children attending and a 300ml glass of squash for him and each of 3 parents who are helping him out. He has 1,040ml of the concentrated squash.

What ratio of water:concentrated squash should he use in the dilution to ensure he has the right amount to go around?

A. 2:1   C. 4:1   E. 6:1

B. 3:1   D. 5:1   F.   5:2

Question 97:

4 children, Alex, Beth, Cathy and Daniel are each sitting on one of the 4 swings in the park. The swings are in a straight line. One possible arrangement of the children is, left to right, Alex, Beth, Cathy, Daniel.

How many other possible arrangements are there?

A. 5   C. 23   E. 64

B. 12   D. 24   F.   256

Question 98:

A delivery driver is looking to make deliveries in several towns. He is given the following map of the various towns in the area. The lines indicate roads between the towns, along with the lengths of these roads.

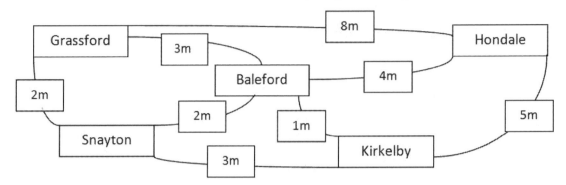

The delivery driver's vehicle has a black box which records the distance travelled and locations visited. At the end of the day, the black box recording shows that he has travelled a total of 14 miles. It also shows that he has visited one town twice, but has not visited any other town more than once. Which of the following is a possible route the driver could have taken?

A. Snayton → Baleford→ Grassford → Snayton→ Kirkelby
B. Baleford → Kirkelby→ Hondale → Grassford→ Baleford→ Snayton
C. Kirkelby → Hondale→ Baleford →Grassford→ Snayton
D. Baleford → Hondale→ Grassford → Baleford→ Hondale→ Kirkelby
E. Snayton → Baleford→ Kirkelby → Hondale→ Grassford
F. None of the above.

Question 99:

Ellie, her brother Tom, her sister Georgia, her mum and her dad line up in height order from shortest to tallest for a family photograph. Ellie is shorter than her dad but taller than her mum. Georgia is shorter than both her parents. Tom is taller than both his parents.

If 1 is shortest and 5 is tallest, what position is Ellie in the line?
A. 1   B. 2   C. 3   D. 4   E. 5

Question 100:

Miss Briggs is trying to arrange the 5 students in her class into a seating plan. Ashley must sit on the front row because she has poor eyesight. Danielle disrupts anyone she sits next to apart from Caitlin, so she must sit next to Caitlin and no-one else. Bella needs to have a teaching assistant sat next to her. The teaching assistant must be sat on the left hand side of the row, near to the teacher. Emily does not get on with Bella, so they need to be sat apart from one another. The teacher has 2 tables which each sit 3 people, which are arranged 1 behind the other.

Who is sitting in the front right seat?
A. Ashley   B. Bella   C. Caitlin   D. Danielle   E. Emily

Question 101:

My aunt runs the dishwasher twice a week, plus an extra time for each person who is living in the house that week. When her son is away at university, she buys a new pack of dishwasher tablets every 6 weeks, but when her son is home she has to buy a new one every 5 weeks. How many people are living in the house when her son is home?

A. 2   C. 4   E. 6
B. 3   D. 5   F. 7

Question 102:

Dates can be written in an 8 digit form, for example 26-12-2014. How many days after 26-12-2014 would be the next time that the 8 digits were made up of exactly 4 different integers?

A. 6
B. 8

C. 10
D. 16

E. 24
F. 30

Question 103:

Redtown is 4 miles east of Greentown. Bluetown is 5 miles north of Greentown. If every town is due North, South, East or West of at least two other towns, and the only other town is Yellowtown, how many miles away from Yellowtown is Redtown, and in what direction?

A. 4 miles east of Yellowtown.
B. 5 miles south of Yellowtown.
C. 5 miles north of Yellowtown.

D. 4 miles west of Yellowtown.
E. 5 miles west of Yellowtown.
F. None of the above.

Question 104:

Jenna pours wine from two 750ml bottles into glasses. The glasses hold 250ml, but she only fills them to 4/5 of capacity, except the last glass, where she puts whatever she has left. How full is the last glass compared to its capacity?

A. 1/5   B. 2/5   C. 3/5   D. 4/5   E. 5/5

Question 105:

There are 30 children in Miss Ellis's class. Two thirds of the girls in Miss Ellis's class have brown eyes, and two thirds of the class as a whole have brown hair. Given that the class is half boys and half girls, what is the difference between the minimum and maximum number of girls that could have brown eyes and brown hair?

A. 0
B. 2

C. 5
D. 7

E. 10
F. More information needed.

Question 106:

A biased die with the numbers 1 to 6 on it is rolled twice. The resulting numbers are multiplied together, and then their sum subtracted from this result to get the 'score' of the dice roll. If the probability of getting a negative (non-zero) score is 0.75, what is the probability of rolling a 1 on a third throw of the die?

A. 0.1
B. 0.2

C. 0.3
D. 0.4

E. 0.5
F. More information needed.

Questions 107 - 109 are based on the following information:

Fares on the number 11 bus are charged at a number of pence per stop that you travel, plus a flat rate. Emma, who is 21, travels 15 stops and pays £1.70. Charlie, who is 43, travels 8 stops and pays £1.14. Children (under 16) pay half the adult flat rate plus a quarter of the adult charge "per stop".

Question 107:

How much does 17 year old Megan pay to travel 30 stops to college?

A. £0.85

B. £2.40

C. £2.90

D. £3.40

E. More information needed.

Question 108:

How much does 14 year old Alice pay to travel 25 stops to school?

A. £0.50

B. £0.75

C. £1.25

D. £2.50

E. More information needed.

Question 109:

James, who is 24, wants to get the bus into town. The town stop is the 25th stop along a straight road from his house, but he only has £2.

Assuming he has to walk past the stop nearest his house, how many stops will he need to walk past before he gets to the stop he can afford to catch the bus from?

A. 4

B. 6

C. 7

D. 8

E. 9

F. 10

Questions 110 -112 are based on the following information:

Emma mounts and frames paintings. Each painting needs a mount which is 2 inches bigger in each dimension than the painting, and a wooden frame which is 1 inch bigger in each dimension than the mount. Mounts are priced by multiplying 50p by the largest dimension of the mount, so a mount which is 8 inches in one direction and 6 in the other would be £4. Frames are priced by multiplying £2 by the smallest dimension of the frame, so a frame which is 8 inches in one direction and 6 in the other would be £12.

Question 110:

How much would mounting and framing a painting that is 10 x 14 inches cost?

A. £8   B. £26   C. £27   D. £34   E. £42

Question 111:

How much more would mounting and framing a 10 x 10 inch painting cost than mounting and framing an 8 x 8 inch painting?

A. £ 3.00   B. £ 4.00   C. £ 5.00   D. £ 6.00   E. £ 7.00

Question 112:

What is the largest square painting that can be framed for £40?

A. 12 inches

B. 13 inches

C. 14 inches

D. 15 inches

E. 16 inches

Question 113:

If the word 'CREATURES' is coded as 'FTEAWUTEV', which itself would be coded as 'HWEAYUWEX'. What would be the second coding of the word 'MAGICAL'?

A. QCKIGAN

B. OCIIEAN

C. PAJIFAN

D. RALIHAQ

E. RCIMGEP

Question 114:

Jane's mum has asked Jane to go to the shops to get some items that they need. She tells Jane that she will pay her per kilometre that she cycles on her bike to get to the shop, plus a flat rate payment for each place she goes to. Jane receives £6 to go to the grocers, a distance of 5 km, and £4.20 to go the supermarket, a distance of 3km.

How much would she earn if she then cycles to the library to change some books, a distance of 7 km?

A. £7.50

B. £7.70

C. £7.80

D. £8.00

E. £8.10

F. £8.20

Question 115:

In 2001-2002, 1,019 patients were admitted to hospital due to obesity. This figure was more than 11 times higher by 2011-12 when there were 11,736 patients admitted to hospital with the primary reason for admission being obesity.

If the rate of admissions due to obesity continues to increase at the same linear rate as it has from 2001/2 to 2011/12, how many admissions would you expect in 2031/32?

A. 22,453

B. 23,437

C. 33,170

D. 134,964

E. 269,928

F. 300,000

Question 116:

A shop puts its dresses on sale at 20% off the normal selling price. During the sale, the shop makes a 25% profit over the price at which they bought the dresses. What is the percentage profit when the dresses are sold at full price?

A. 36%

B. 42.5%

C. 56.25%

D. 64%

E. 77%

F. 80%

Question 117:

The 'Keys MedSoc committee' is made up of 20 students from each of the 6 years at the university. However, the president and vice-president are sabbatical roles (students take a year out from studying). There must be at least two general committee students from each year, as well as the specialist roles. Additionally, the social and welfare officers must be pre-clinical students (years 1-3) but not first years, and the treasurer must be a clinical student (years 4-6).

Which **TWO** of the following statements must be true?

1. There can be a maximum of 13 preclinical (years 1-3) students on the committee.
2. There must be a minimum of 6 2nd and 3rd years.
3. There is an unequal distribution of committee members over the different year groups.
4. There can be a maximum of 10 clinical (years 4-6) students on the committee.
5. There can be a maximum of 2 first year students on the committee.
6. General committee members are equally spread across the 6 years.

A. 1 and 4

B. 2 and 3

C. 2 and 4

D. 3 and 6   E. 4 and 5   F. 4 and 6

Question 118:

Friday the 13th is superstitiously considered an 'unlucky' day. If 13th January 2012 was a Friday, when would the next Friday the 13th be?

A. March 2012   E. July 2012
B. April 2012   F. August 2012
C. May 2012   G. September 2012
D. June 2012   H. January has the only Friday 13th in 2012.

Question 119:

A farmer has 18 sheep, 8 of which are male. Unfortunately, 9 sheep die, of which 5 were female. The farmer decides to breed his remaining sheep in order to increase the size of his herd. Assuming every female gives birth to two lambs, how many sheep does the farmer have after all the females have given birth once?

A. 10   B. 14   C. 15   D. 16   E. 19

Question 120:

Piyanga writes a coded message for Nishita. Each letter of the original message is coded as a letter a specific number of characters further on in the alphabet (the specific number is the same for all letters). Piyanga's coded message includes the word "PJVN". What could the original word say?

A. CAME   B. DAME   C. FAME   D. GAME   E. LAME

Question 121:

A number of people get on the bus at the station, which is considered the first stop. At each subsequent stop, 1/2 of the people on the bus get off and then 2 people get on. Between the 4th and 5th stop after the station, there are 5 people on the bus.

How many people got on at the station?

A. 4   B. 6   C. 20   D. 24   E. 30

Question 122:

I have recently moved into a new house, and I am looking to repaint my new living room. The price of several different colours of paint is displayed in the table below. A small can contains enough to paint 10 m² of wall. A large can contains enough to paint 25 m² of wall.

Colour	Cost for a Small Can	Cost for a Large Can
Red	£4	£12
Blue	£8	£15
Black	£3	£9
White	£2	£13
Green	£7	£15
Orange	£5	£20
Yellow	£10	£12

I decide to paint my room a mixture of blue and white, and I purchase some small cans of blue paint and white paint. The cost of blue paint accounts for 50% of the total cost. I paint a total of 100 m² of wall space.

I use up all the paint. How many m² of wall space have I painted blue?

A. 10 m²   B. 20 m²   C. 40 m²   D. 50 m²   E. 80 m²

Question 123:

Cakes usually cost 42p at the bakers. The bakers want to introduce a new offer where the amount in pence you pay for each cake is discounted by the square of the number of cakes you buy. For example, buying 3 cakes would mean each cake costs 33p. Isobel says that this is not a good offer from the baker's perspective as it would be cheaper to buy several cakes than just 1. How many cakes would you have to buy for the total cost to fall below 40p?

A. 2   B. 3   C. 4   D. 5   E. 6

Question 124:

The table below shows the percentages of students in two different universities who take various courses. There are 800 students in University A and 1200 students in University B. Biology, Chemistry and Physics are counted as "Sciences".

	University A	University B
Biology	23.50	13.25
Economics	10.25	14.5
Physics	6.25	14.75
Mathematics	11.50	17.25
Chemistry	30.25	7.00
Psychology	18.25	33.25

Assuming each student only takes one course, how many more students in University A than University B study a "Science"?

A. 10   B. 25   C. 60   D. 250   E. 600

Question 125:

Traveleasy Coaches charge passengers at a rate of 50p per mile travelled, plus an additional charge of £5.00 for each international border crossed during the journey. Europremier Coaches charge £15 for every journey, plus 10p per mile travelled, with no charge for crossing international borders. Sonia is travelling from France to Germany, crossing 1 international border. She finds that both companies will charge the same price for this journey.

How many miles is Sonia travelling?

A. 10   B. 20   C. 25   D. 35   E. 40

Question 126:

Lauren, Amy and Chloe live in different cities across England. They decide to meet up together in London and have a meal together. Lauren departs from Southampton at 2:30pm, and arrives in London at 4pm. Amy's journey lasts twice as long as Lauren's journey and she arrives in London at 4:15pm. Chloe departs from Sheffield at 1:30pm, and her journey lasts an hour longer than Lauren's journey.

Which of the following statements is definitely true?

A. Chloe's journey took the longest time.
B. Amy departed after Lauren.
C. Chloe arrived last.
D. Everybody travelled by train.
E. Amy departed before Chloe.

Question 127:

Emma is packing to go on holiday by aeroplane. On the aeroplane, she can take a case of dimension 50cm by 50cm by 20cm, which, when fully packed, can weigh up to 20kg. The empty suitcase weighs 2kg. In her suitcase, she needs to take 3 books, each of which is 0.2m by 0.1m by 0.05m in size, and weighs 1000g. She would also like to take as many items of clothing as possible. Each item of clothing has volume 1500cm³ and weighs 400 g.

Assuming each item of clothing can be squashed so as to fill any shape gap, how many items of clothing can she take in her case?

A. 28   B. 31   C. 34   D. 37   E. 40

Question 128:

Alex is buying a new bed and mattress. There are 5 bed shops Alex can buy the bed and mattress he wants from, each of which sells the bed and mattress for a different price as follows:
➤ **Bed Shop A:** Bed £120, Mattress £70
➤ **Bed Shop B:** All beds and mattresses £90 each
➤ **Bed Shop C:** Bed £140, Mattress £60. Mattress half price when you buy a bed and mattress together.
➤ **Bed Shop D:** Bed £140, Mattress £100. Get 33% off when you buy a bed and mattress together.
➤ **Bed Shop E:** Bed £175. All beds come with a free mattress.

Which is the cheapest place for Alex to buy the bed and mattress from?
A. Bed Shop A   C. Bed Shop C   E. Bed Shop E
B. Bed Shop B   D. Bed Shop D

Question 129:

In Joseph's sock drawer, there are 21 socks. 4 are blue, 5 are red, 6 are green and the rest are black. How many socks does he need to take from the drawer in order to guarantee he has a matching pair?
A. 3   B. 4   C. 5   D. 6   E. 7

Question 130:

Printing a magazine uses 1 sheet of card and 25 sheets of paper. It also uses ink. Paper comes in packs of 500 and card comes in packs of 60 which are twice the price of a pack of paper. Each ink cartridge prints 130 sheets of either paper or card. A pack of paper costs £3. Ink cartridges cost £5 each.

How many complete magazines can be printed with a budget of £300?
A. 210   B. 220   C. 230   D. 240   E. 250

Question 131:

Rebecca went swimming yesterday. After a while she had covered one fifth of her intended distance. After swimming six more lengths of the pool, she had covered one quarter of her intended distance. How many lengths of the pool did she intend to complete?
A. 40   B. 72   C. 80   D. 100   E. 120

Question 132:

As a special treat, Sammy is allowed to eat five sweets from his very large jar which contains many sweets of each of three flavours – Lemon, Orange and Strawberry. He wants to eat his five sweets in such a way that no two consecutive sweets have the same flavour.

In how many ways can he do this?

A. 32   B. 48   C. 72   D. 108   E. 162

Question 133:

Granny and her granddaughter Gill both had their birthday yesterday. Today, Granny's age in years is an even number and 15 times that of Gill. In 4 years' time Granny's age in years will be the square of Gill's age in years.

How many years older than Gill is Granny today?

A. 42   B. 49   C. 56   D. 60   E. 64

Question 134:

Pierre said, "Just one of us is telling the truth". Qadr said, "What Pierre says is not true". Ratna said, "What Qadr says is not true". Sven said, "What Ratna says is not true". Tanya said, "What Sven says is not true".

How many of them were telling the truth?

A. 0   B. 1   C. 2   D. 3   E. 4

Question 135:

Two entrants in a school's sponsored run adopt different tactics. Angus walks for half the time and runs for the other half, whilst Bruce walks for half the distance and runs for the other half. Both competitors walk at 3 mph and run at 6 mph. Angus takes 40 minutes to complete the course.

How many minutes does Bruce take?

A. 30   B. 35   C. 40   D. 45   E. 50

Question 136:

Dr Song discovers two new alien life forms on Mars. Species 8472 have one head and two legs. Species 24601 have four legs and one head. Dr Song counts a total of 73 heads and 290 legs in the area. How many members of Species 8472 are present?

A. 0   C. 72   E. 145
B. 1   D. 73   F. More information needed.

Question 137:

A restaurant menu states that:

"All chicken dishes are creamy and all vegetable dishes are spicy. No creamy dishes contain vegetables."

Which of the following **must** be true?

A.   Some chicken dishes are spicy.
B.   All spicy dishes contain vegetables.
C.   Some creamy dishes are spicy.
D.   Some vegetable dishes contain tomatoes.
E.   None of the above

Question 138:

Simon and his sister Lucy both cycle home from school. One day, Simon is kept back in detention so Lucy sets off for home first. Lucy cycles the 8 miles home at 10 mph. Simon leaves school 20 minutes later than Lucy. How fast must he cycle in order to arrive home at the same time as Lucy?

A. 10 mph   B. 14 mph   C. 17 mph   D. 21 mph   E. 24 mph

Question 139:

Dr. Whu buys 2000 shares in a company at a rate of 50p per share. He then sells the shares for 58p per share. Subsequently he buys 1000 shares at 55p per share then sells them for 61p per share. There is a charge of £20 for each transaction of buying or selling shares. What is Dr. Whu's total profit?

A. £140   B. £160   C. £180   D. £200   E. £220

Question 140:

Jina is playing darts. A dartboard is composed of equal segments, numbered from 1 to 20. She takes three throws, and each of the darts lands in a numbered segment. None land in the centre or in double or triple sections. What is the probability that her total score with the three darts is odd?

A. $\frac{1}{4}$ B. $\frac{1}{3}$ C. $\frac{1}{2}$ D. $\frac{3}{5}$ E. $\frac{2}{3}$

Question 141:

John Morgan invests £5,000 in a savings bond paying 5% interest per annum. What is the value of the investment in 5 years' time?

A. £6,250   B. £6,315   C. £6,381   D. £6,442   E. £6,570

Question 142:

Joe is 12 years younger than Michael. In 5 years the sum of their ages will be 62. How old was Michael two years ago?

A. 20   B. 24   C. 26   D. 30   E. 32

Question 143:

A book has 500 pages. Vicky tears every page out that is a multiple of 3. She then tears out every remaining page that is a multiple of 6. Finally, she tears out half of the remaining pages. If the book measures 15 cm x 30cm and is made from paper of weight 110 gm^{-2}, how much lighter is the book now than at the start?

A. 1,648 g   B. 1,698 g   C. 1,722 g   D. 1,790 g   E. 1,848 g

Question 144:

A farmer is fertilising his crops. The more fertiliser is used, the more the crops grow. Fertiliser costs 80p per kilo. Fertilising at a rate of 0.2 kgm^{-2} increases the crop yield by £1.30 m^{-2}. For each additional 100g of fertiliser above 200g, the extra yield is 30% lower than the linear projection of the stated rate. At what rate of fertiliser application is it no longer cost effective to increase the dose

A. 0.5 kgm^{-2} B. 0.6 kgm^{-2} C. 0.7 kgm^{-2} D. 0.8 kgm^{-2} E. 0.9 kgm^{-2}

Question 145:

Pet-Star, Furry Friends and Creature Cuddles are three pet shops, which each sell food for various types of pets.

Type of pet food	Amount of food required per week	Price per Kg in:		
		Pet-star	Furry Friends	Creature Cuddles
Guinea Pig	3 Kg	£2	£1	£1.50
Cat	6 Kg	£4	£6	£5
Rabbit	4 Kg	£3	£1	£2.50
Dog	8 Kg	£5	£8	£6
Chinchilla	2 Kg	£1.50	£0.50	£1

Given the information above, which of the following statements can we state is definitely *not* true?

A. Regardless of which of these shops you use, the most expensive animal to provide food for will be a dog.
B. If I own a mixture of cats and rabbits, it will be cheaper for me to shop at Pet-star.
C. If I own 3 cats and a dog, the cheapest place for me to shop is at Pet-star
D. Furry Friends sells the cheapest food for the type of pet requiring the most food
E. If I only have one pet, Creature Cuddles will not be the cheapest place to shop regardless of which type of pet I have.

Question 146:

I record my bank balance at the start of each month for six months to help me see how much I am spending each month. My salary is paid on the 10th of each month. At the start of the year, I earn £1000 a month but from March inclusive I receive a pay rise of 10%.

Date	Bank balance
January 1st	1,200
February 1st	1,029
March 1st	1,189
April 1st	1,050
May 1st	925
June 1st	1,025

In which month did I spend the most money?
A. January
B. February
C. March
D. April
E. May

Question 147:

Amy needs to travel from Southtown station to Northtown station, which are 100 miles apart. She can travel by 3 different methods: train, aeroplane or taxi. The tables below show the different times for these 3 methods. The taxi takes 1 minute to cover a distance of 1 mile. Aeroplane passengers must be at the airport 30 minutes before their flight. Southtown airport is 10 minutes travelling time from Southtown station and Northtown airport is 30 minutes travelling time from Northtown station.

If Amy wants to arrive by 1700 and wants to set off as late as possible, what method of travel should she choose and what time will she leave Southtown station?

Train	Departs Southtown station	1400	1500	1600
	Arrives Northtown station	1615	1650	1715
Flights	Departs Southtown airport	1610		
	Arrives Northtown airport	1645		

A. Flight, 1530
B. Train, 1600
C. Taxi, 1520
D. Train, 1500
E. Flight, 1610

Question 148:

In the multiplication grid below, a, b, c and d are all integers. What does d equal?

	c	d
a	168	720
b	119	510

A. 18
B. 24
C. 30
D. 40
E. 45

Question 149:

A sixth form college has 1,500 students. 48% are girls. 80 of the girls are mixed race.

If an equal proportion of boys and girls are mixed race, how many mixed race boys are there in the college to the nearest 10?

A. 50
B. 60
C. 70
D. 80
E. 90

Question 150:

Christine is a control engineer at the Browdon Nuclear Power Plant. On Wednesday, she is invited to a party on the Friday, and asks her manager if she can take the Friday off. She acknowledged that this will mean she will have worked less than the required number of hours this week, and offers to make this up by working extra hours next week. Her manager suggests that instead, she works 5 hours this Sunday, and 3 extra hours next Thursday to make up the required hours. Christine accepts this proposal. Christine's amended schedule for the week is shown below:

Day	Monday	Tuesday	Wednesday	Thursday	Friday	Saturday	Sunday
Hours worked	8	7	9	6	0	0	5

How many hours was Christine supposed to have worked this week, if she had completed her usual Friday shift?

A. 34
B. 35
C. 36
D. 38
E. 40
F. 42

Question 151:

Leonidas notes that the time on a normal analogue clock is 0340. What is the smaller angle between the hands on the clock?

A. 110°
B. 120°
C. 130°
D. 140°
E. 150°

Question 152:

Sheila is on a shift at the local supermarket. Unfortunately, the till has developed a fault, meaning it cannot tell her how much change to give each customer. A customer is purchasing the following items, at the following costs:

- A packet of grated cheese priced at £3.25
- A whole cucumber, priced at 75p
- A fish pie mix, priced at £4.00
- 3 DVDs, each priced at £3.00

Sheila knows there is an offer on DVDs in the store at present, in which 3 DVDs bought together will only cost £8.00.The customer pays with a £50 note. How much change will Sheila need to give the customer?

A. £33
B. £34
C. £35
D. £36
E. £37

SECTION 1A: Data Analysis

Data analysis questions show a great variation in type and difficulty. The best way to improve with these questions is to do lots of practice questions in order to familiarise yourself with the style of questions.

Options First

Despite the fact that you may have lots of data to contend with, the rule about looking at the options first still stands in this section. This will allow you to register what type of calculation you are required to make and what data you might need to look at for this. Remember, Options → Question → Data/Passage.

Working with Numbers

Percentages frequently make an appearance in this section and it's vital that you're able to work comfortably with them. For example, you should be comfortable increasing and decreasing by percentages, and working out inverse percentages too. When dealing with complex percentages, break them down into their components. For example, 17.5% = 10% + 5% + 2.5%.

Graphs and Tables

When you're working with graphs and tables, it's important that you take a few seconds to check the following before actually extracting data from it.

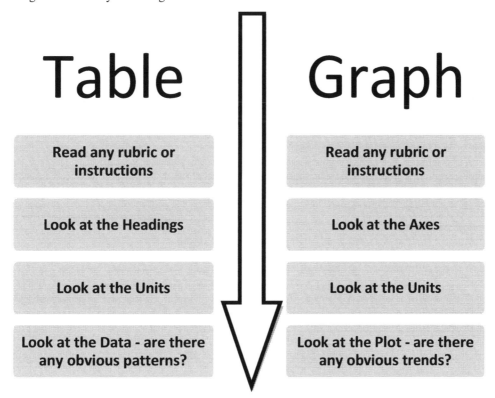

Get into the habit of doing this whenever you are faced with data and you'll find it much easier to approach these questions under time pressure.

Data Analysis Questions

Questions 153 to 155 are based on the following passage:

It has recently been questioned as to whether the recommended five fruit and vegetables a day is sufficient or if it would be more beneficial to eat 7 fruit and vegetable portions each day. A study at UCL looked at the fruit and vegetables eating habits of 65,000 people in England. Analysis of the data showed that eating more portions was beneficial and vegetables seemed to have a greater protective effect than fruit. The study however did not distinguish whether vegetables themselves have a greater protective effect, or whether these people tend to eat an overall healthier diet. A meta-analysis carried out by researchers across the world complied data from 16 studies which encompassed over 800,000 participants, of whom 56,423 had died.

They found a decline in death of around 5% from all causes for each additional portion of fruit or vegetables eaten, however they recorded no further decline for people who ate over 5 portions. Rates of cardiovascular disease, heart disease or stroke, were shown to decline 4% for each portion up to five, whereas the number of portions of fruit and vegetables eaten seemed to have little impact on cancer rates. The data from these studies points in a similar direction, that eating as much fruit and vegetables a day is preferable, but that five portions is sufficient to have a significant impact on reduction in mortality. Further studies need to look into the slight discrepancies, particularly why the English study found vegetables more protective, and if any specific cancers may be affected by fruit and vegetables even if the general cancer rates more greatly depend on other lifestyle factors.

Question 153:

Which of the following statements is correct?

A. The UCL study found no additional reduction in mortality in those who eat 7 rather than 5 portions of fruit and vegetables a day.
B. People who eat more fruit and vegetables are assumed to have an overall healthier diet which is what gives them the beneficial effect.
C. The meta analysis found fruit and vegetables are more protective against cancer than cardiovascular disease
D. The English study showed fruit had more protective effects than vegetables.
E. The meta-analysis found no additional reduction in mortality in those who eat 7 rather than 5 portions of fruit and vegetables a day.
F. The meta-analysis suggests people who eat 7 portions would have a 10% lower risk of death from any cause than those who eat 5 portions.
G. Fruit and vegetables are not protective against any specific cancers.

Question 154:

If rates of death were found to be 1% lower in the UCL study than the meta-analysis, approximately how many people died in the UCL study?

A. 3,000   B. 3,200   C. 3,900   D. 4,550   E. 5,200

Question 155:

Which statement does the article **MOST** agree with?

A. Eating more fruit and vegetables does not particularly lower the risk of any specific cancers.
B. The UCL research suggests that the guideline should be 7 fruit and vegetables a day for England.
C. The results found by the UCL study and the meta-analysis were contradictory.
D. Many don't eat enough vegetables due to cost and taste.
E. Fruit and vegetables are only protective against cardiovascular disease.
F. The UCL study and meta-analysis use a similar sample of participants.

G. People should aim to eat 7 portions of fruit and vegetables a day.

Questions 156-258 relate to the following table regarding average alcohol consumption in 2010.

Country	Total	Recorded Consumption	Unrecorded consumption	Beer (%)	Wine (%)	Spirits (%)	Other (%)	2020 Consumption Projection
Belarus		14.4	3.2	17.3	5.2	46.6	30.9	17.1
Lithuania	15.4	12.9	2.5		7.8	34.1	11.6	16.2
Andorra	13.8		1.4	34.6		20.1	0	9.1
Grenada	12.5	11.9	0.7	29.3	4.3		0.2	10.4
Czech Republic	13	11.8	1.2	53.5	20.5	26	0	14.1
France	12.2	11.8		18.8	56.4	23.1	1.7	11.6
Russia		11.5	3.6	37.6	11.4	51	0	14.5
Ireland	11.9	11.4	0.5	48.1	26.1	18.7	7.7	10.9

NB: Some data is missing.

Question 156:

Which of the following countries had the highest total beer and wine consumption for 2010?

A. Belarus
B. Lithuania
C. Ireland
D. France
E. Andorra

Question 157:

Which country has the greatest difference for spirit consumption in 2010 and 2020 projection, assuming percentages stay the same?

A. Russia
B. Belarus
C. Lithuania
D. Grenada
E. Ireland

Question 158:

It was later found that some of the percentages of types of alcohol consumed had been mixed up. If the actual amount of beer consumed by each person in the Czech Republic was on average 4.9L, which country were the percentage figures mixed up with?

A. Lithuania
B. Grenada
C. Russia
D. France
E. Ireland
F. Belarus
G. Andorra

Questions 159-162 are based on the following information:

The table below shows the incidence of 6 different types of cancer in Australia:

	Prostate	Lung	Bowel	Bladder	Breast	Uterus
Men	40,000	25,000	20,000	8,000	1,000	0
Women	0	20,000	18,000	4,000	50,000	9,000

Question 159:

Supposing there are 10 million men and 10 million women in Australia, how many percentage points higher is the incidence of cancer amongst women than amongst men?

A. 0.007 %   B. 0.07 %   C. 0.093 %   D. 0.7 %   E. 0.93 %

Question 160:

Now suppose there are 11.5 million men and 10 million women in Australia. Assuming all men are equally likely to get each type of cancer and all women are equally likely to get each type of cancer, how many of the types of cancer are you more likely to develop if you are a man than if you are a woman?

A. 1   B. 2   C. 3   D. 4

Question 161:

Suppose that prostate, bladder and breast cancer patients visit hospital 1 time during the first month of 2015 and patients for all other cancers visit hospital 2 times during the first month of 2015. 10% of cancer patients in Australia are in Sydney, and patients in Sydney are not more or less likely to have certain types of cancer than other patients.

How many hospital visits are made by patients in Sydney with these 6 cancers during the first month of 2015?

A. 10,300   C. 19,500   E. 195,000

B. 18,400   D. 28,700   F. 287,000

Question 162:

Which of the graphs correctly represents the combined proportion of men versus women with bladder cancer?

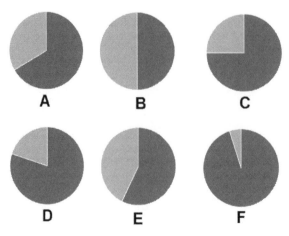

Questions 163 – 165 are based on the following information:

Units of alcohol are calculated by multiplying the alcohol percentage by the volume of liquid in litres, for example a 0.75 L bottle of wine which is 12% alcohol contains 9 units. 1 pint = 570 ml.

	Volume in bottle/barrel	Standard drinks per bottle/barrel	Percentage
Vodka	1250 ml	50	40%
Beer	10 pints	11.4	3%
Cocktail	750 ml	3	8%
Wine	750 ml	3.75	12.5%

Question 163:

Which standard drink has the most units of alcohol in?

A. Vodka
B. Beer
C. Cocktail
D. Wine

Question 164:

Some guidance suggests the recommended maximum number of units of alcohol per week for women is 14. In a week, Hannah drinks 4 standard drinks of wine, 3 standard drinks of beer, 2 standard cocktails and 5 standard vodkas. This guidance states the recommended maximum number of units per week for men is 21. In a week, Mark drinks 2 standard drinks of wine, 6 standard drinks of beer, 3 standard cocktails and 10 standard vodkas.

Who has exceeded their recommended maximum number of units by more and by how many units more have they exceeded it by than the other person?

A. Hannah, by 1 unit
B. Hannah, by 0.5 units
C. Both by the same
D. Mark, by 0.5 units
E. Mark, by 1 unit

Question 165:

How many different combinations of drinks that total 4 units are there (the same combination in a different order doesn't count).

A. 2
B. 3
C. 4
D. 5
E. 6

Questions 166-168 relate to the table below which shows information about Greentown's population:

	Female	Male	Total
Under 20	1,930		
20-39	1,960	3,760	5,720
40-59		4,130	
60 and over	2,350	2,250	4,600
Total	11,430	12,890	24,320

Question 166:

How many males under 20 are there in Greentown?

A. 2,650
B. 2,700
C. 2,730
D. 2,750
E. 2,850

Question 167:

How many females aged 40-59 are there in Greentown?

A. Between 3,000 and 4,000
B. Between 4,000 and 5,000
C. Between 5,000 and 6,000
D. Between 6,000 and 7,000

Question 168:

Which is the approximate ratio of females:males in the age group that has the highest ratio of males:females?

A. 1.4:1
B. 1.9:1
C. 1:1.9
D. 1:1.4

Questions 169-171 relate to the follow graph:

The graph below shows the average temperatures in London (top trace) and Newcastle (bottom trace).

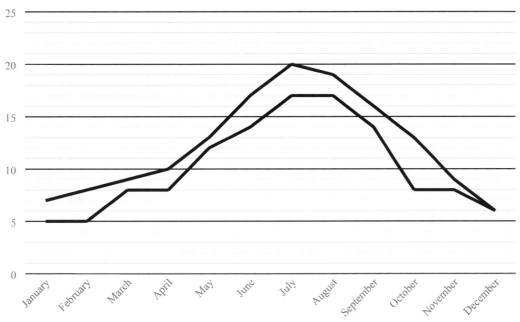

Question 169:

If the average monthly temperature is the same in every year, how many times during the period May 2007 to September 2013 inclusive is the average temperature the same in 2 consecutive months in Newcastle?

A. 20
B. 24
C. 25
D. 30

Question 170:

In how many months in the period specified in the previous question is the average temperature in London AND Newcastle lower than the previous month?

A. 19
B. 21
C. 25
D. 32

Question 171:

To the nearest 0.5 degrees Celcius, what is the average temperature difference between Newcastle and London?

A. 1.5°C
B. 2°C
C. 2.5 °C
D. 3 °C

Questions 172-174 concern the following data:

The pie chart to the right shows sales of ice cream across the four quarters of a year from January to December. Sales are lowest in the month of February. From February they increase in every subsequent month until they get to the maximum sales and from that point they decrease in every subsequent month until the end of the year.

Sales of ice cream

Question 172:

In which month are the sales highest?

A. June   B. July   C. August   D. Cannot tell

Question 173:

If total sales of ice cream were £354,720 for the year, how much of this was taken during Q1?

A. 29,480   B. £29,560   C. £29,650   D. £29,720   E. £29,800

Question 174:

Assuming total sales revenue (i.e. before costs are taken off) is £180,000, and that each tub of ice cream is sold for £2 and costs the manufacturer £1.50 in total production and transportation costs, how much profit is made during Q2?

A. £15,000   B. £30,000   C. £45,000   D. £60,000

Question 175:

Data on the amount families spend on food per month to the nearest £100 was collected for families with 1, 2 and 3 children. The percentage of families with different spending sizes is displayed below:

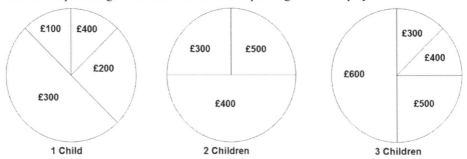

Which of the following statements is definitely true?

A. More families with 1 child than families with 2 children spent £300 a month on food.
B. The overall fraction of families spending £600 was 1/6.
C. All of the families with 2 children spent under £4000 on food per year.
D. The fraction of families with 1 child spending £400 on food per month is the same as the fraction of families with 3 children spending this amount.
E. The average amount spent on food by families with 2 children is £410 a month.

Questions 176-179 are based on the passage below:

A big secondary school recently realised that there were a large number of incidences of bullying occurring that were going unnoticed by teachers. It is possible that some believe bullying to be as much a part of student life as lessons and homework. In order to tackle the problem, the school emailed out a questionnaire to all students' parents and asked them to question their children about where they had experienced or seen bullying in school. Those children that answered yes were then asked if they had told their teachers about it, and asked why they did not if they had not. Those that had told their teacher were asked whether they had seen the teacher act upon the information and whether the bullying had stopped as a result.

Of the 2500 school students surveyed 2210 filled in the online questionnaire. The results were that, 1121 students, almost exactly half (50.7%) had seen bullying in school. Only 396 (35%) of these students told a teacher about the bullying. Of the students who told a teacher, 286 did not witness any action following sharing of the information and of those that did, 60% did not notice any direct action with the bully involved. From those students who did not report the bullying, 146 gave the reason that they didn't think it was important. 427 cited fears of being found out. 212 students said they did not tell because they didn't think the teachers would do anything about it even if they did know. Assume that all the students who filled out the survey did so honestly.

Question 176:
To the nearest integer, what percentage of students did not respond?
A. 10%   B. 12%   C. 18%   D. 8%   E. 5%

Question 177:
If a student saw bullying occur and did not tell a teacher about it, what is the probability that the reasoning for this is that they thought it to be unimportant?

A. 0.1   B. 0.15   C. 0.2   D. 0.35   E. 0.13

Question 178:
After reporting the bullying, how many students saw the teacher act on the information directly with the bully?

A. 66
B. 44
C. 178
D. 104
E. 118

Question 179:
Which of the following does the questionnaire indicate is the best explanation for why students at the school did not report bullying?

A. Students do not think bullying happens at their school.
B. Students think the teachers will do nothing with the information.
C. Students think that bullying is a part of school life.
D. The student's were worried about others finding out.

Question 180:

The obesity epidemic is growing rapidly with reports of a three-fold rise in the period from 2007 to 2012. The rates of hospital admission have also been found to vary massively across different areas of England with the highest rates in the North-East (56 per 100,000 people), and the lowest rates in the East of England (12 per 100,000). During almost every year from 2001-12, there were around twice as many women admitted for obesity as men. The reason for this is however unclear and does not imply there are twice as many obese women as men.

What was the approximate number of admissions per 100 000 women in the North-East in 2011-12?

A. 18   B. 26   C. 37   D. 56   E. 62   F. 74

Question 181:

Health professionals are becoming increasingly worried by the decline in exercise being taken by both children and adults. Around only 40% of adults take the recommended amount of exercise which is 150 minutes per week. As well as falling rates of exercise, a shockingly low number of individuals eat five portions of fruit and vegetables a day. Figures for children aged 5-15 fell to only 16% for boys, and 20% for girls in 2011. Data for adults was only slightly better with 29% of women and 24% of men eating the recommended number of portions.

Using a figure of 8 million children between 5-15 years (equal ratio of girls to boys) in England in 2011, how many more girls than boys ate 5 portions of fruit and vegetables a day?

A. 80,000   B. 120,000   C. 160,000   D. 320,000   E. 640,000

Question 182:

The table below shows the leading causes of death in the UK.

Rank	WOMEN		MEN	
	Cause of Death	**Number of Deaths**	**Cause of Death**	**Number of Deaths**
1	Dementia and Alzheimer's	31,850	Coronary Heart Disease	37,797
2	Coronary Heart Disease	26,075	Lung Cancer	16,818
3	Stroke	20,706	Dementia and Alzheimer's	15,262
4	Flu and Pneumonia	15,361	Lower Respiratory Disease	15,021
5	Lower Respiratory Disease	14,927	Stroke	14,058
6	Lung Cancer	13,619	Flu and Pneumonia	11,426
7	Breast Cancer	10,144	Prostate Cancer	9,726
8	Colon Cancer	6,569	Colon Cancer	7,669
9	Urinary Infections	5,457	Lymphatic Cancer	6,311
10	Heart Failure	5,012	Liver Disease	4,661
	Total	**261,205**	**Total**	**245,585**

Using information from the table only, which of the following statements is correct?

A. More women died from cancers than men.

B. More than 30,000 women died due to respiratory causes.

C. Dementia and Alzheimer's is more common in women than men.

D. No cause of death is of the same ranking for both men and women.

Question 183 is based on the passage below:

The government has recently released a campaign leaflet saying that last year waiting times in NHS A&E departments decreased 20% compared to the year before. The opposition has criticised this statement, saying that there are several definitions which can be described as "waiting times", and the government's campaign leaflet does not make it clear what they mean by "waiting times in A&E".

The NHS watchdog has recently released the following figures describing different aspects of A&E departments, and the change from last year:

Assessment Criterion	2014	2013
Average time spent before being seen in A&E	1 hour	90 minutes
Average time between dialling 999 and receiving treatment in A&E	2 hours	3 hours
Number of people waiting for over 4 hours in A&E	3200	4000
Number of high-priority cases waiting longer than 1 hour	900	1000
Average waiting time for those seen in under 4 hours	50 minutes	40 minutes

Question 183:

Assuming these figures are correct, which criterion of assessment have the government described as "waiting times in A&E" on their campaign leaflet?

A. Number of people waiting for over 4 hours in A&E.

B. Number of people waiting for under 4 hours in A&E.

C. Number of high-priority cases waiting longer than 1 hour.

D. Average time spent before being seen in A&E.

E. Average time between dialling 999 and receiving treatment in A&E.

F. Average waiting time for those seen in less than 4 hours.

Questions 184– 186 refer to the following information:

The table below shows the final standings at the end of the season, after each team has played all the other teams twice each (once at home, once away). The teams are listed in order of how many points they got during the season. Teams get 3 points for a win, 1 point for a draw and 0 points for a loss. No team got the same number of points as another team. Some of the information in the table is missing.

Team	W	D	L
United	8	1	
Athletic	7		
City	7	2	
Town	1	4	
Rovers		0	9
Rangers		2	8

Question 184:

How many points did Rovers get?

A. 0
B. 3
C. 6
D. 9
E. More information needed.

Question 185:

How many games did Athletic lose?

A. 0
B. 1
C. 2
D. 3
E. More information needed.

Question 186:

How many more points did United get than Rangers?

A. 7
B. 15
C. 23
D. 25
E. More information needed.

Questions 187-189 use information from the graph recording A&E attendances and response times for NHS England from 2004 to 2014. Type 1 departments are major A&E units, type 2&3 are urgent care centres or minor injury units. The old target (2004 – June 2010) was 97.5%; the new target (July 2010 – 2015) is 95%.

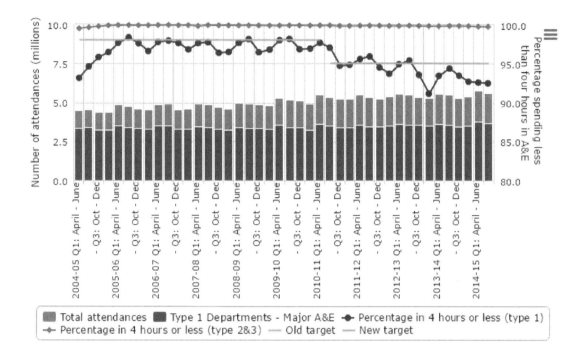

Question 187:

Which of the following statements is **FALSE**?

A. There has been an overall increase in total A&E attendances from 2004-2014.
B. The number of attendances in type 1 departments has been fairly constant from 2004-2014.
C. The new target of 4 hours waiting time has only been reached in two quarters by type 1 departments.
D. The change in attendances is largely due to an in increase people going to type 2&3 departments.

Question 188:

What percentage has the number of total attendances changed from Q1 2004-5 to Q1 2008-9?

A. +5%   C. +10%   E. +15%
B. –5%   D. –10%   F. –15%

Question 189:

If the new target was achieved by type 1 departments 4 times, in what percentage of the quarters was the target missed?

A. 25%
B. 60%
C. 75%
D. 90%

Questions 190-191 relate to the following data:

Ranjna is travelling from Manchester to Bali. She is required to make a stopover in Singapore for which he wants to allow at least 2 hours. It takes 14 hours to fly from Manchester to Singapore, and 2 hours from Singapore to Bali. The table below shows the departure times in local time [Manchester GMT, Singapore GMT + 8, Bali GMT + 8]:

Manchester to Singapore				Singapore to Bali			
Monday	Wednesday	Thursday	Monday	Tuesday	Wednesday	Thursday
08.00	09.30	02.30	13.00	00.00	15.30	13.00
10.45	14.00	08.30	15.30	07.30	18.00	16.00
13.30	18.00	12.30	21.00	08.30	20.30	19.00
15.00	20.00	19.00		12.00		

Question 190:

What is the latest flight Ranjna can take from Manchester to ensure she arrives at Bali Airport by Thursday 22:00?

A. 18:00 Tuesday
B. 14:00 Wednesday
C. 18:00 Wednesday
D. 20:00 Wednesday
E. 02:30 Thursday
F. 08:30 Thursday

Question 191:

Ranjna takes the 08:00 flight from Manchester to Singapore on Monday. She allows 1 hour to clear customs and collect her luggage at Bali Airport and another 45 minutes for the taxi to her hotel. At what time will she arrive at the hotel?

A. 16.45 Monday
B. 04:15 Tuesday
C. 10:30 Tuesday
D. 12:15 Tuesday
E. 12:30 Tuesday
F. 20:30 Tuesday

Question 192:

The graph below represents the percentage of adult smokers in the UK from 1974 to 2010. The top trace represents men and the bottom trace represents women. The middle trace is for both men and women.

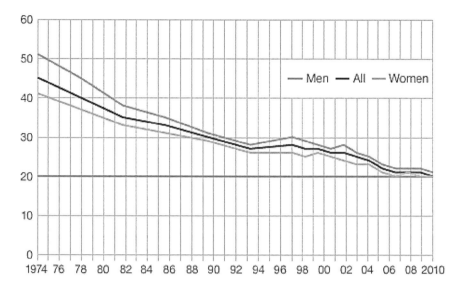

Which of the following statements can be concluded from the graph?

A. The 2007 smoking ban increased the rate in decline of smokers.
B. There has been a constant reduction in percentage of smoker since 1974.
C. The highest rate in decline in smoking for women was 2004-2006.
D. From 1974 to 2010, the smoking rate in men decreased by a half.
E. There has always been a significant difference between the smoking habits of men and women.

Question 193:

The name, age, height, weight and IQ of 11 people were recorded below in a table and a scatter plot. However, the axis labels were left out by mistake.   Scale breaks are permitted.

Name	Age	Height (cm)	Weight (kg)	IQ
Alice	18	180	68	110
Ben	12	160	79	120
Camilla	14	170	62	100
David	25	145	98	108
Eliza	29	165	75	96
Rohan	15	190	92	111
George	20	172	88	104
Hannah	22	168	68	115
Ian	13	182	86	98
James	17	176	90	102
Katie	27	151	66	125

Which variants are possible for the X and Y axis?

	X axis	Y axis
A	Height	Weight
B	IQ	Height
C	Age	IQ
D	Height	IQ

E	Height	Age
F	IQ	Weight

Question 194:

A group of students looked at natural variation in height and arm span within their group and got the following results:

Name	Arm span (cm)	Height (cm)
Adam	175	168
Tom	188	175
Shiv	172	184
Mary	148	142
Alice	165	156
Sarah	166	168
Emily	159	160
Matthew	165	172
Michael	185	183

They then drew a scatter plot, but forgot to include names for each point. They also forgot to plot one student.

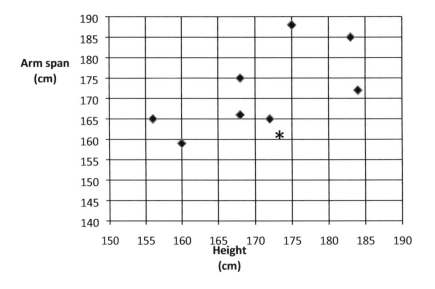

Which student is represented by the point marked with a *?

A. Alice
B. Sarah
C. Matthew
D. Adam
E. Emily
F. Michael

Questions 195 - 201 are based on the following information:

The rectangle represents women. The circle represents those that have children. The triangle represents those that work, and the square those that went to university.

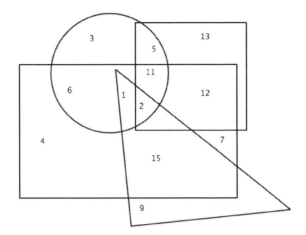

Question 195:

What is the number of non-working women who have children and who did not go to university?

A. 3   B. 5   C. 6   D. 7   E. 9

Question 196:

What is the total number of women who have children and work?

A. 1   B. 2   C. 3   D. 11   E. 14

Question 197:

How many women were surveyed in total?

A. 49   C. 58   E. 85
B. 51   D. 67   F. None of the above.

Question 198:

What is the number of people who went to university and had children?

A. 5   C. 13   E. 18
B. 11   D. 16   F. None of the above.

Question 199:

What is the total number of people who went to university, or have children but not both?

A. 18   C. 35   E. 53
B. 28   D. 41   F. None of the above.

Question 200:

The total number of men who went to university and had children was?

A. 3   B. 4   C. 5   D. 12   E. 13   F. 18

Question 201:

Which of the following people were not surveyed? Choose **TWO** options.

A. A non-working woman who went to university but did not have children.
B. A working man who went to university and has children.
C. A working woman who had children but did not go to university.
D. A non-working man who did not have children and did not go to university.
E. A working woman who went to university but did not have children.

Question 202:

Savers"R"Us is national chain of supermarkets. The price of several items in the supermarket is displayed below:

Item	Price
Beef roasting joint	£8.00
Chicken breast fillet	£6.00
Lamb shoulder	£7.00
Pork belly meat portion	£4.00
Sausages – 10 pack	£3.50

This week the supermarket has a sale on, with 50% off the normal price of all meat products. Alfred visits the supermarket during this sale and purchases a beef roasting joint, a 10 pack of sausages and a lamb shoulder, paying with a £20 note.

How much change does Alfred get?

A. £1.50   C. £10.75   E. £12.50
B. £5.00   D. £11.75   F. None of the above.

Question 203:

The local football league table is shown below, but the number of goals scored against Wilmslow is missing. Each team played the other teams in the league once at home and once away during the season.

Team Name	Points	Goals For	Goals Against
Sale	20	16	2
Wilmslow	16	11	?
Timperley	14	8	7
Altrincham	13	7	9
Mobberley	10	8	12
Hale	8	4	14

How many goals must Wilmslow have conceded?

A. 8   C. 10   E. 12
B. 9   D. 11   F. 14

Question 204:

The heights and weights of three women with BMI's 21, 22 and 23 were measured. If Julie and Lydia had different weights but the same height of 154 cm, and the weight of Emma, Lydia and Julie combined was 345 lbs, what was Emma's height?

Weight (lbs)

		100	105	110	115	120
	152	19	20	22	24	26
	154	18	19	21	23	25
	156	17	18	20	22	24
	158	15	17	19	21	23
Height	**160**	14	15	18	20	22
(cm)	**162**	13	14	17	19	21
	164	12	13	15	18	20
	166	11	12	14	17	19
	168	10	11	13	15	18
	170	9	10	12	14	17

A. 158 cm
B. 162 cm
C. 160 cm
D. 164 cm
E. 165 cm

Question 205:

The measurements for different types of fish appear below:

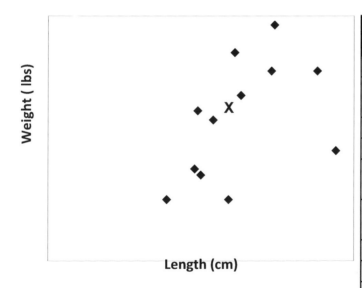

	Length (cm)	Weight (lbs)
Bluecup	78	40
Silverfinn	96	60
Starbug	98	98
Jawless	100	56
Lamprene	108	92
Scarfynne	118	40
Rayfish	122	136
Lobefin	126	108
Eringill	146	124
Whaler	148	154
Magic fish	176	124
Blondeye	188	72

Which fish is shown by the point marked **X**?

A. Silverfinn   C. Lobefin   E. Eringill
B. Starbug   D. Blondeye

The following graphs are required for questions 206-207:

The graph below shows the price of crude oil in US Dollars during 2014:

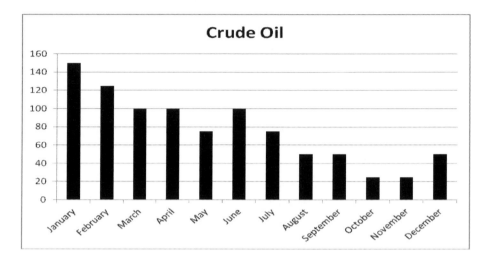

The graph below shows total oil production, in millions of barrels per day:

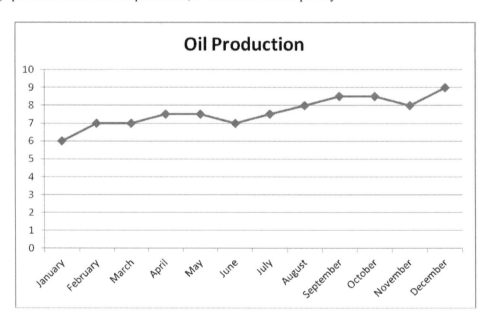

Question 206:

What was approximate total oil production in 2014?

A.   1,750 million barrels

B.   2,146 million barrels

C.   2,300 million barrels

D.   2,700 million barrels

E.   3,500 million barrels

Question 207:

How much did oil sales total in July 2014?

A. $0.56 Billion   B. $16.9 Billion   C. $17.4 Billion   D. $21.1 Billion

SECTION 1B: Advanced Maths

Section 1B tests principles of advanced mathematics. You have to answer 15 questions in 40 minutes. The questions can be quite difficult and it's easy to get bogged down. However, it's well worth spending time preparing for this section as its possible to rapidly improve with targeted preparation.

Gaps in Knowledge

You are highly advised to go through the ECAA Specification and ensure that you have covered all examinable topics. An electronic copy of this can be obtained from **uniadmissions.co.uk/ecaa.** The questions in this book will help highlight any particular areas of weakness or gaps in your knowledge that you may have. Upon discovering these, make sure you take some time to revise these topics before carrying on – there is little to be gained by attempting these questions with huge gaps in your knowledge. A summary of the major topics is given below:

Algebra:
➢ Laws of Indices
➢ Manipulation of Surds
➢ Quadratic Functions: Graphs, use of discrimiant, completing the square
➢ Solving Simulatenous Equations via Substitution
➢ Solving Linear and Quadratic Inequalities
➢ Manipulation of polynomials e.g. expanding brackets, factorising
➢ Use of Factor Theorem + Remainder Theorem

Graphing Functions:
➢ Sketching of common functions including lines, quadratics, cubics, trigonometric functions, logarithmic functions and exponential functions
➢ Manipulation of functions using simple transformaions

Exponentials & Logs:
➢ Graph of $y = a^x$ series
➢ Law of Lograithms:
  - $a^b = c \leftrightarrow b = log_a c$
  - $log_a x + log_a y = log_a(xy)$
  - $log_a x - log_a y = log_a\left(\frac{x}{y}\right)$
  - $k \, log_a x = log_a(x^k)$
  - $log_a\frac{1}{x} = -log_a x$
  - $log_a a = 1$

Trignometry:
➢ Sine and Cosine rules
➢ Solution of trigonometric identities
➢ Values of sin, cost, tan for 0, 30, 45, 60 and 90 degrees
➢ Sine, Cosine, Tangent graphs, symmetries, perioditicties
➢ $Area \; of \; Triangle = \frac{1}{2}ab\sin C$
➢ $\sin^2 \theta + \cos^2 \theta = 1$
➢ $tan\theta = \frac{sin\theta}{\cos \theta}$

Differentiation:

➢ First order and second order derivatives

➢ Familiarity with notation: $\frac{dy}{dx}, \frac{d^2y}{dx^2}, f'(x), f''(x)$

➢ Differentiation of functions like $y = x^n$

Integration:

➢ Definite and indefinite integrals for $y = x^n$

➢ Solving Differential Equations in the form: $\frac{dy}{dx} = f(x)$

➢ Understanding of the Fundamental Theorem of Calculus and its application:

o $$\int_a^b f(x)dx = F(b) - F(a), where \; F'(x) = f(x)$$

o $$\frac{d}{dx}\int_a^x f(t)dt = f(x)$$

Geometry:

➢ Circle Properties:
  o The angle subtended by an arc at the centre of a circle is double the size of the angle subtended by the arc on the circumference
  o The opposite angles in a cyclic quadrilateral summate to 180 degrees
  o The angle between the tanent and chord at the point of contact is equal to the angle in the alternate segment
  o The tangent at any point on a circle is perpendicular to the radius at that point
  o Triangles formed using the full diameter are right-angled triangles
  o Angles in the same segment are equal
  o The Perpendicular from the centre to a chord bisects the chord
➢ Equations for a circle:
  o $(x - a)^2 + (y - b)^2 = r^2$
  o $x^2 + y^2 + cx + dy + e = 0$
➢ Equations for a straight line:
  o $y - y_1 = m(x - x_1)$
  o $Ax + by + c = 0$

Series:

➢ Arithmetic series and Geometric Series
➢ Summing to a finite and infinite geometric series
➢ Binomial Expansions
➢ Factorials

Logic Arguments:

➢ Terminology: True, flase, and, or not, necessary, sufficient, for all, for some, there exists.
➢ Arguments in the format:
  o If A then B
  o A if B
  o A only if B
  o A if and only if B

Formulas you **MUST** know:

2D Shapes		3D Shapes		
Area			**Surface Area**	**Volume**
Circle	πr^2	**Cuboid**	Sum of all 6 faces	Length x width x height
Parallelogram	Base x Vertical height	**Cylinder**	$2\pi r^2 + 2\pi rl$	πr^2 x l
Trapezium	0.5 x h x (a+b)	**Cone**	$\pi r^2 + \pi rl$	πr^2 x (h/3)
Triangle	0.5 x base x height	**Sphere**	$4\pi r^2$	$(4/3)\pi r^3$

Even good students who are studying maths at A level can struggle with certain ECAA maths topics because they're usually glossed over at school. These include:

Quadratic Formula

The solutions for a quadratic equation in the form $ax^2 + bx + c = 0$ are given by:
$$x = \frac{-b \pm \sqrt{b^2 - 4ac}}{2a}$$

Remember that you can also use the discriminant to quickly see if a quadratic equation has any solutions:

If $b^2 - 4ac < 0$:No solutions
If $b^2 - 4ac = 0$:One solution
If $b^2 - 4ac > 2$:Two solutions

Completing the Square

If a quadratic equation cannot be factorised easily and is in the format $ax^2 + bx + c = 0$ then you can rearrange it into the form $a\left(x + \frac{b}{2a}\right)^2 + [c - \frac{b^2}{4a}] = 0$

This looks more complicated than it is – remember that in the ECAA, you're extremely unlikely to get quadratic equations where $a > 1$ and the equation doesn't have any easy factors. This gives you an easier equation:

$\left(x + \frac{b}{2}\right)^2 + \left[c - \frac{b^2}{4}\right] = 0$ and is best understood with an example.

Consider: $x^2 + 6x + 10 = 0$

This equation cannot be factorised easily but note that: $x^2 + 6x - 10 = (x + 3)^2 - 19 = 0$

Therefore, $x = -3 \pm \sqrt{19}$. Completing the square is an important skill – make sure you're comfortable with it.

Difference between 2 Squares

If you are asked to simplify expressions and find that there are no common factors but it involves square numbers – you might be able to factorise by using the 'difference between two squares'.

For example, $x^2 - 25$ can also be expressed as $(x + 5)(x - 5)$.

Maths Questions

Questions 208 – 282 are easier than you will get in the exam but have been included for practice.

Question 208:

Robert has a box of building blocks. The box contains 8 yellow blocks and 12 red blocks. He picks three blocks from the box and stacks them up high. Calculate the probability that he stacks two red building blocks and one yellow building block, in **any** order.

A. $\dfrac{8}{20}$ B. $\dfrac{44}{95}$ C. $\dfrac{11}{18}$ D. $\dfrac{8}{19}$ E. $\dfrac{12}{20}$ F. $\dfrac{35}{60}$

Question 209:

Solve $\dfrac{3x+5}{5}+\dfrac{2x-2}{3}=18$

A. 12.11   B. 13.49   C. 13.95   D. 14.2   E. 19   F. 265

Question 210:

Solve $3x^2+11x-20=0$

A. 0.75 and $-\dfrac{4}{3}$

B. -0.75 and $\dfrac{4}{3}$

C. -5 and $\dfrac{4}{3}$

D. 5 and $\dfrac{4}{3}$

E. 12 only

F. -12 only

Question 211:

Express $\dfrac{5}{x+2}+\dfrac{3}{x-4}$ as a single fraction.

A. $\dfrac{15x-120}{(x+2)(x-4)}$

B. $\dfrac{8x-26}{(x+2)(x-4)}$

C. $\dfrac{8x-14}{(x+2)(x-4)}$

D. $\dfrac{15}{8x}$

E. 24

F. $\dfrac{8x-14}{x^2-8}$

Question 212:

The value of p is directly proportional to the cube root of q. When p = 12, q = 27. Find q when p = 24.

A. 32   B. 64   C. 124   D. 128   E. 216   F. 1728

Question 213:

Write 72^2 as a product of its prime factors.

A. $2^6 \times 3^4$ C. $2^4 \times 3^4$ E. $2^6 \times 3$

B. $2^6 \times 3^5$ D. 2×3^3 F. $2^3 \times 3^2$

Question 214:

Calculate: $\dfrac{2.302 \times 10^5 + 2.302 \times 10^2}{1.151 \times 10^{10}}$

A. 0.0000202   C. 0.00002002   E. 0.000002002

B. 0.00020002   D. 0.00000002   F. 0.000002002

Question 215:

Given that $y^2 + \mathbf{a}y + \mathbf{b} = (y + 2)^2 - 5$, find the values of **a** and **b**.

	a	b
A	-1	4
B	1	9
C	-1	-9
D	-9	1
E	4	-1
F	4	1

Question 216:

Express $\dfrac{4}{5} + \dfrac{m - 2n}{m + 4n}$ as a single fraction in its simplest form:

A. $\dfrac{6m + 6n}{5(m + 4n)}$ C. $\dfrac{20m + 6n}{5(m + 4n)}$ E. $\dfrac{3(3m + 2n)}{5(m + 4n)}$

B. $\dfrac{9m + 26n}{5(m + 4n)}$ D. $\dfrac{3m + 9n}{5(m + 4n)}$ F. $\dfrac{6m + 6n}{3(m + 4n)}$

Question 217:

A is inversely proportional to the square root of B. When A = 4, B = 25.

Calculate the value of A when B = 16.

A. 0.8   B. 4   C. 5   D. 6   E. 10   F. 20

Question 218:

S, T, U and V are points on the circumference of a circle, and O is the centre of the circle.

Given that angle SVU = 89°, calculate the size of the smaller angle SOU.

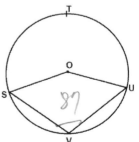

A. 89°   B. 91°   C. 102°   D. 178°   E. 182°   F. 212°

Question 219:

Open cylinder A has a surface area of 8π cm^2 and a volume of 2π cm^3. Open cylinder B is an enlargement of A and has a surface area of 32π cm^2. Calculate the volume of cylinder B.

A. 2π cm^3 C. 10π cm^3 E. 16π cm^3

B. 8π cm^3 D. 14π cm^3 F. 32π cm^3

Question 220:

Express $\dfrac{8}{x(3-x)} - \dfrac{6}{x}$ in its simplest form.

A. $\dfrac{3x-10}{x(3-x)}$

B. $\dfrac{3x+10}{x(3-x)}$

C. $\dfrac{6x-10}{x(3-2x)}$

D. $\dfrac{6x-10}{x(3+2x)}$

E. $\dfrac{6x-10}{x(3-x)}$

F. $\dfrac{6x+10}{x(3-x)}$

Question 221:

A bag contains 10 balls. 9 of those are white and 1 is black. What is the probability that the black ball is drawn in the tenth and final draw if the drawn balls are not replaced?

A. 0

B. $\dfrac{1}{10}$

C. $\dfrac{1}{100}$

D. $\dfrac{1}{10^{10}}$

E. $\dfrac{1}{362,880}$

Question 222:

Gambit has an ordinary deck of 52 cards. What is the probability of Gambit drawing 2 Kings (without replacement)?

A. 0

B. $\dfrac{1}{169}$

C. $\dfrac{1}{221}$

D. $\dfrac{4}{663}$

E. None of the above

Question 223:

I have two identical unfair dice, where the probability that the dice get a 6 is twice as high as the probability of any other outcome, which are all equally likely. What is the probability that when I roll both dice the total will be 12?

A. 0

B. $\dfrac{4}{49}$

C. $\dfrac{1}{9}$

D. $\dfrac{2}{7}$

E. None of the above

Question 224:

A roulette wheel consists of 36 numbered spots and 1 zero spot (i.e. 37 spots in total).
What is the probability that the ball will stop in a spot either divisible by 3 or 2?

A. 0   B. $\dfrac{25}{37}$ C. $\dfrac{25}{36}$ D. $\dfrac{18}{37}$ E. $\dfrac{24}{37}$

Question 225:

I have a fair coin that I flip 4 times. What is the probability I get 2 heads and 2 tails?

A. $\dfrac{1}{16}$

B. $\dfrac{3}{16}$

C. $\dfrac{3}{8}$

D. $\dfrac{9}{16}$

E. None of the above

Question 226:

Shivun rolls two fair dice. What is the probability that he gets a total of 5, 6 or 7?

A. $\dfrac{9}{36}$

B. $\dfrac{7}{12}$

C. $\dfrac{1}{6}$

D. $\dfrac{5}{12}$

E. None of the above

Question 227:

Dr Savary has a bag that contains x red balls, y blue balls and z green balls (and no others). He pulls out a ball, replaces it, and then pulls out another. What is the probability that he picks one red ball and one green ball?

A. $\dfrac{2(x+y)}{x+y+z}$

B. $\dfrac{xz}{(x+y+z)^2}$

C. $\dfrac{2xz}{(x+y+z)^2}$

D. $\dfrac{(x+z)}{(x+y+z)^2}$

E. $\dfrac{4xz}{(x+y+z)^4}$

F. More information needed

Question 228:

Mr Kilbane has a bag that contains x red balls, y blue balls and z green balls (and no others). He pulls out a ball, does **NOT** replace it, and then pulls out another. What is the probability that he picks one red ball and one blue ball?

A. $\dfrac{2xy}{(x+y+z)^2}$

B. $\dfrac{2xy}{(x+y+z)(x+y+z-1)}$

C. $\dfrac{2xy}{(x+y+z)^2}$

D. $\dfrac{xy}{(x+y+z)(x+y+z-1)}$

E. $\dfrac{4xy}{(x+y+z-1)^2}$

F. More information needed

Question 229:

There are two tennis players. The first player wins the point with probability p, and the second player wins the point with probability 1-p. The rules of tennis say that the first player to score four points wins the game, unless the score is 4-3. At this point the first player to get two points ahead wins.

What is the probability that the first player wins in exactly 5 rounds?

A. $4p^4(1-p)$ C. $4p(1-p)$ E. $4p^5(1-p)$

B. $p^4(1-p)$ D. $4p(1-p)^4$ F. More information needed

Question 230:

Solve the equation $\dfrac{4x + 7}{2} + 9x + 10 = 7$

A. $\dfrac{22}{13}$ B. $-\dfrac{22}{13}$ C. $\dfrac{10}{13}$ D. $-\dfrac{10}{13}$ E. $\dfrac{13}{22}$ F. $-\dfrac{13}{22}$

Question 231:

The volume of a sphere is $V = \dfrac{4}{3}\pi r^3$, and the surface area of a sphere is $S = 4\pi r^2$. Express S in terms of V

A. $S = (4\pi)^{2/3}(3V)^{2/3}$ D. $S = (4\pi)^{1/3}(3V)^{2/3}$

B. $S = (8\pi)^{1/3}(3V)^{2/3}$ E. $S = (16\pi)^{1/3}(9V)^{2/3}$

C. $S = (4\pi)^{1/3}(9V)^{2/3}$

Question 232:

Express the volume of a cube, V, in terms of its surface area, S.

A. $V = (S/6)^{3/2}$ D. $V = (S/6)^{1/2}$

B. $V = S^{3/2}$ E. $V = (S/36)^{1/2}$

C. $V = (6/S)^{3/2}$ F. $V = (S/36)^{3/2}$

Question 233:

Solve the equations $4x + 3y = 7$ and $2x + 8y = 12$

A. $(x,y) = \left(\dfrac{17}{13}, \dfrac{10}{13}\right)$

B. $(x,y) = (\dfrac{10}{13}, \dfrac{17}{13})$

C. $(x,y) = (1, 2)$
D. $(x,y) = (2, 1)$
E. $(x,y) = (6, 3)$
F. $(x,y) = (3, 6)$
G. No solutions possible.

Question 234:

Rearrange $\dfrac{(7x + 10)}{(9x + 5)} = 3y^2 + 2$, to make x the subject.

A. $\dfrac{15\,y^2}{7 - 9(3y^2 + 2)}$ C. $-\dfrac{15\,y^2}{7 - 9(3y^2 + 2)}$ E. $-\dfrac{5\,y^2}{7 + 9(3y^2 + 2)}$

B. $\dfrac{15\,y^2}{7 + 9(3y^2 + 2)}$ D. $-\dfrac{15\,y^2}{7 + 9(3y^2 + 2)}$ F. $\dfrac{5\,y^2}{7 + 9(3y^2 + 2)}$

Question 235:

Simplify $3x\left(\dfrac{3x^7}{x^{\frac{1}{3}}}\right)^3$

A. $9x^{20}$ B. $27x^{20}$ C. $87x^{20}$ D. $9x^{21}$ E. $27x^{21}$ F. $81x^{21}$

Question 236:

Simplify $2x[(2x)^7]^{\frac{1}{14}}$

A. $2x\sqrt{2\,x^4}$ C. $2\sqrt{2\,x^4}$ E. $8x^3$
B. $2x\sqrt{2x^3}$ D. $2\sqrt{2x^3}$ F. $8x$

Question 237:

What is the circumference of a circle with an area of 10π?

A. $2\pi\sqrt{10}$

B. $\pi\sqrt{10}$

C. 10π

D. 20π

E. $\sqrt{10}$

F. More information needed

$2\pi r$

$\pi r^2 =$

$r = \sqrt{10}$

Question 238:

If $a.b = (ab) + (a+b)$, then calculate the value of $(3.4).5$

A. 19

B. 54

C. 100

D. 119

E. 132

$12 + 7 = 19$

$95 + 24$

Question 239:

If $a.b = \dfrac{a^b}{a}$, calculate $(2.3).2$

A. $\dfrac{16}{3}$

B. 1

C. 2

D. 4

E. 8

$\dfrac{2^3}{2} = 4$

$4.2 =$

Question 240:

Solve $x^2 + 3x - 5 = 0$

$-3 \pm \sqrt{9+20}$

A. $x = -\dfrac{3}{2} \pm \dfrac{\sqrt{11}}{2}$

B. $x = \dfrac{3}{2} \pm \dfrac{\sqrt{11}}{2}$

C. $x = -\dfrac{3}{2} \pm \dfrac{\sqrt{11}}{4}$

D. $x = \dfrac{3}{2} \pm \dfrac{\sqrt{11}}{4}$

E. $x = \dfrac{3}{2} \pm \dfrac{\sqrt{29}}{2}$

F. $x = -\dfrac{3}{2} \pm \dfrac{\sqrt{29}}{2}$

Question 241:

How many times do the curves $y = x^3$ and $y = x^2 + 4x + 14$ intersect?

A. 0

B. 1

C. 2

D. 3

E. 4

$16 -$

Question 242:

Which of the following graphs **do not** intersect?

1. $y = x$

2. $y = x^2$

3. $y = 1 - x^2$

4. $y = 2$

A. 1 and 2

B. 2 and 3

C. 3 and 4

D. 1 and 3

E. 1 and 4

F. 2 and 4

Question 243:

Calculate the product of 897,653 and 0.009764.

A. 87646.8

B. 8764.68

C. 876.468

D. 87.6468

$900,000$

0.001

0.01

E.   8.76468   F.   0.876468

Question 244:

Solve for x: $\dfrac{7x+3}{10} + \dfrac{3x+1}{7} = 14$

A. $\dfrac{929}{51}$ B. $\dfrac{949}{47}$ C. $\dfrac{949}{79}$ D. $\dfrac{980}{79}$

Question 245:

What is the area of an equilateral triangle with side length x.

A. $\dfrac{x^2\sqrt{3}}{4}$ B. $\dfrac{x\sqrt{3}}{4}$ C. $\dfrac{x^2}{2}$ D. $\dfrac{x}{2}$ E. x^2
                                                                    F. x

Question 246:

Simplify $3 - \dfrac{7x(25x^2-1)}{49x^2(5x+1)}$

A. $3 - \dfrac{5x-1}{7x}$ C. $3 + \dfrac{5x-1}{7x}$ E. $3 - \dfrac{5x^2}{49}$

B. $3 - \dfrac{5x+1}{7x}$ D. $3 + \dfrac{5x+1}{7x}$ F. $3 + \dfrac{5x^2}{49}$

Question 247:

Solve the equation $x^2 - 10x - 100 = 0$

A. $-5 \pm 5\sqrt{5}$ C. $5 \pm 5\sqrt{5}$ E. $5 \pm 5\sqrt{125}$
B. $-5 \pm \sqrt{5}$ D. $5 \pm \sqrt{5}$ F. $-5 \pm \sqrt{125}$

Question 248:

Rearrange $x^2 - 4x + 7 = y^3 + 2$ to make x the subject.

A. $x = 2 \pm \sqrt{y^3 + 1}$
B. $x = 2 \pm \sqrt{y^3 - 1}$
C. $x = -2 \pm \sqrt{y^3 - 1}$
D. $x = -2 \pm \sqrt{y^3 + 1}$
E. x cannot be made the subject for this equation.

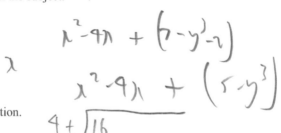

Question 249:

Rearrange $3x + 2 = \sqrt{7x^2 + 2x + y}$ to make y the subject.

A. $y = 4x^2 + 8x + 2$ C. $y = 2x^2 + 10x + 2$ E. $y = x^2 + 10x + 2$
B. $y = 4x^2 + 8x + 4$ D. $y = 2x^2 + 10x + 4$ F. $y = x^2 + 10x + 4$

Question 250:

Rearrange $y^4 - 4y^3 + 6y^2 - 4y + 2 = x^5 + 7$ to make y the subject.

A. $y = 1 + (x^5 + 7)^{1/4}$

B. $y = -1 + (x^5 + 7)^{1/4}$

C. $y = 1 + (x^5 + 6)^{1/4}$

D. $y = -1 + (x^5 + 6)^{1/4}$

Question 251:

The aspect ratio of my television screen is 4:3 and the diagonal is 50 inches. What is the area of my television screen?

30×40

A. 1,200 inches^2

B. 1,000 inches^2

C. 120 inches^2

D. 100 inches^2

1200

E. More information needed.

Question 252:

Rearrange the equation $\sqrt{1 + 3x^{-2}} = y^5 + 1$ to make x the subject.

A. $x = \dfrac{(y^{10} + 2y^5)}{3}$

$1 + \dfrac{3}{x^2} = y^{10} + 2y^5 + 1$

B. $x = \dfrac{3}{(y^{10} + 2y^5)}$

$\dfrac{3}{y^{10} + 2y^5}$

C. $x = \sqrt{\dfrac{3}{y^{10} + 2y^5}}$

D. $x = \sqrt{\dfrac{y^{10} + 2y^5}{3}}$

E. $x = \sqrt{\dfrac{y^{10} + 2y^5 + 2}{3}}$

F. $x = \sqrt{\dfrac{3}{y^{10} + 2y^5 + 2}}$

Question 253:

Solve $3x - 5y = 10 \text{ and } 2x + 2y = 13$.

$6x - 10y = 10$

$6x + 6y = 39$

$16y = 19$

A. $(x,y) = (\dfrac{19}{16}, \dfrac{85}{16})$

B. $(x,y) = (\dfrac{85}{16}, -\dfrac{19}{16})$

C. $(x,y) = (\dfrac{85}{16}, \dfrac{19}{16})$

D. $(x,y) = (-\dfrac{85}{16}, -\dfrac{19}{16})$

E. No solutions possible.

Question 254:

The two inequalities $x + y \leq 3 \text{ and } x^3 - y^2 < 3$ define a region on a plane. Which of the following points is inside the region?

A. (2, 1)

B. (2.5, 1)

C. (1, 2)

D. (3, 5)

E. (1, 2.5)

F. None of the above.

Question 255:

How many times do $y = x + 4 \text{ and } y = 4x^2 + 5x + 5$ intersect?

16—

A. 0

B. 1

C. 2

D. 3

E. 4

$9n^2 + 9n + 1$

$16 - 16$

Question 256:

How many times do $y = x^3$ and $y = x$ intersect?

A. 0   B. 1 C. 2   D. 3   E. 4

Question 257:

A cube has unit length sides. What is the length of a line joining a vertex to the midpoint of the opposite side?

A. $\sqrt{2}$

B. $\sqrt{\dfrac{3}{2}}$

C. $\sqrt{3}$

D. $\sqrt{5}$

E. $\dfrac{\sqrt{5}}{2}$

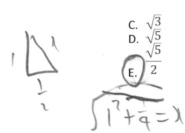

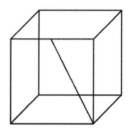

Question 258:

Solve for x, y, and z.

1. $x + y - z = -1$
2. $2x - 2y + 3z = 8$
3. $2x - y + 2z = 9$

	x	y	z
A	2	-15	-14
B	15	2	14
C	14	15	-2
D	-2	15	14
E	2	-15	14
F	No solutions possible		

Question 259:

Fully factorise: $3a^3 - 30a^2 + 75a$

A. $3a(a - 3)^3$

B. $a(3a - 5)^2$

C. $3a(a^2 - 10a + 25)$

D. $3a(a - 5)^2$

E. $3a(a + 5)^2$

Question 260:

Solve for x and y:

$4x + 3y = 48$

$3x + 2y = 34$

(handwritten: $8x + 6y = 96$, $9x + 6y = 102$, $x = 6$)

	x	y
A	8	6
B	6	8
C	3	4
D	4	3
E	30	12
F	12	30
G	No solutions possible

Question 261:

Evaluate: $\dfrac{-(5^2 - 4 \times 7)^2}{-6^2 + 2 \times 7}$

A. $-\dfrac{3}{50}$

B. $\dfrac{11}{22}$

C. $-\dfrac{3}{22}$

D. $\dfrac{9}{50}$

E. $\dfrac{9}{22}$

F. 0

Question 262:

All license plates are 6 characters long. The first 3 characters consist of letters and the next 3 characters of numbers. How many unique license plates are possible?

A. 676,000

B. 6,760,000

C. 67,600,000

D. 1,757,600

E. 17,576,000

F. 175,760,000

Question 263:

How many solutions are there for: $2(2(x^2 - 3x)) = -9$

A. 0

B. 1

C. 2

D. 3

E. Infinite solutions.

Question 264:

Evaluate: $\left(x^{\frac{1}{2}} y^{-3}\right)^{\frac{1}{2}}$

A. $\dfrac{x^{\frac{1}{2}}}{y}$

B. $\dfrac{x}{y^{\frac{3}{2}}}$

C. $\dfrac{x^{\frac{1}{4}}}{y^{\frac{3}{2}}}$

D. $\dfrac{y^{\frac{1}{4}}}{x^{\frac{3}{2}}}$

Question 265:

Bryan earned a total of £ 1,240 last week from renting out three flats. From this, he had to pay 10% of the rent from the 1-bedroom flat for repairs, 20% of the rent from the 2-bedroom flat for repairs, and 30% from the 3-bedroom flat for repairs. The 3-bedroom flat costs twice as much as the 1-bedroom flat. Given that the total repair bill was £ 276 calculate the rent for each apartment.

	1 Bedroom	2 Bedrooms	3 Bedrooms
A	280	400	560
B	140	200	280
C	420	600	840
D	250	300	500
E	500	600	1,000

Question 266:

Evaluate: $5\,[5(6^2 - 5\,x\,3) + 400^{\frac{1}{2}}]^{1/3} + 7$

A. 0　　　　B. 25　　　　C. 32　　　　D. 49　　　　E. 56　　　　F. 200

Question 267:

What is the area of a regular hexagon with side length 1?

A. $3\sqrt{3}$

B. $\dfrac{3\sqrt{3}}{2}$

C. $\dfrac{\sqrt{3}}{\sqrt{3}}$

D. $\dfrac{\sqrt{3}}{2}$

E. 6

F. More information needed

Question 268:

Dexter moves into a new rectangular room that is 19 metres longer than it is wide, and its total area is 780 square metres. What are the room's dimensions?

A. Width = 20 m; Length = -39 m

B. Width = 20 m; Length = 39 m

C. Width = 39 m; Length = 20 m

D. Width = -39 m; Length = 20 m

E. Width = -20 m; Length = 39 m

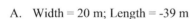

Question 269:

Tom uses 34 meters of fencing to enclose his rectangular lot. He measured the diagonals to 13 metres long. What is the length and width of the lot?

A. 3 m by 4 m

B. 5 m by 12 m

C. 6 m by 12 m

D. 8 m by 15 m

E. 9 m by 15 m

F. 10 m by 10 m

Question 270:

Solve $\dfrac{3x - 5}{2} + \dfrac{x + 5}{4} = x + 1$

A. 1

B. 1.5

C. 3

D. 3.5

E. 4.5

F. None of the above

Question 271:

Calculate: $\dfrac{5.226 \times 10^6 + 5.226 \times 10^5}{1.742 \times 10^{10}}$

A. 0.033

B. 0.0033

C. 0.00033

D. 0.000033

E. 0.0000033

Question 272:

Calculate the area of the triangle shown to the right:

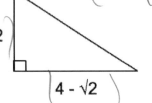

A. $\dfrac{3 + \sqrt{2}}{2 + 2\sqrt{2}}$

B. $\dfrac{2}{2}$

C. $2 + 5\sqrt{2}$

D. $3 - \sqrt{2}$

E. 3

F. 6

Question 273:

Rearrange $\sqrt{\dfrac{4}{x} + 9} = y - 2$ to make x the subject.

A. $x = \dfrac{11}{(y - 2)^2}$

B. $x = \dfrac{9}{(y - 2)^2}$

C. $x = \dfrac{4}{(y + 1)(y - 5)}$

D. $x = \dfrac{4}{(y - 1)(y + 5)}$

E. $x = \dfrac{4}{(y + 1)(y + 5)}$

F. $x = \dfrac{4}{(y - 1)(y - 5)}$

Question 274:

When 5 is subtracted from 5x the result is half the sum of 2 and 6x. What is the value of x?

A. 0

B. 1

C. 2

D. 3

E. 4

F. 6

Question 275:

Estimate $\dfrac{54.98 + 2.25^2}{\sqrt{905}}$

A. 0

B. 1

C. 2

D. 3

E. 4

F. 5

Question 276:

At a Pizza Parlour, you can order single, double or triple cheese in the crust. You also have the option to include ham, olives, pepperoni, bell pepper, meat balls, tomato slices, and pineapples. How many different types of pizza are available at the Pizza Parlour?

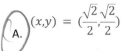

A. 10   C. 192   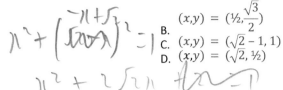 E. 768

B. 96   D. 384   F. None of the above

Question 277:

Solve the simultaneous equations $x^2 + y^2 = 1$ *and* $x + y = \sqrt{2}$, for x, y > 0

A. $(x,y) = (\frac{\sqrt{2}}{2}, \frac{\sqrt{2}}{2})$

B. $(x,y) = (\frac{1}{2}, \frac{\sqrt{3}}{2})$
C. $(x,y) = (\sqrt{2} - 1, 1)$
D. $(x,y) = (\sqrt{2}, \frac{1}{2})$

Question 278:

Which of the following statements is **FALSE**?

A. Congruent objects always have the same dimensions and shape.

B. Congruent objects can be mirror images of each other.

C. Congruent objects do not always have the same angles.

D. Congruent objects can be rotations of each other.

E. Two triangles are congruent if they have two sides and one angle of the same magnitude.

Question 279:

Solve the inequality $x^2 \geq 6 - x$

A. $x \leq -3$ and $x \leq 2$ C. $x \geq -3$ and $x \leq 2$ E. $x \geq 2$ only

B. $x \leq -3$ and $x \geq 2$ D. $x \geq -3$ and $x \geq 2$ F. $x \geq -3$ only

Question 280:

The hypotenuse of an ~~equilateral~~ right-angled triangle is x cm. What is the area of the triangle in terms of x?

A. $\frac{\sqrt{x}}{2}$ B. $\frac{x^2}{4}$ C. $\frac{x}{4}$ D. $\frac{3x^2}{4}$ E. $\frac{x^2}{10}$

Question 281:

Mr Heard derives a formula: $Q = \frac{(X + Y)^2 A}{3B}$. He doubles the values of X and Y, halves the value of A and triples the value of B. What happens to value of Q?

A. Decreases by $\frac{1}{3}$ C. Decreases by $\frac{2}{3}$ E. Increases by $\frac{4}{3}$

B. Increases by $\frac{1}{3}$ D. Increases by $\frac{2}{3}$ F. Decreases by $\frac{4}{3}$

Question 282:

Consider the graphs $y = x^2 - 2x + 3$, and $y = x^2 - 6x - 10$. Which of the following is true?

A. Both equations intersect the x-axis.

B. Neither equation intersects the x-axis.

C. The first equation does not intersect the x-axis; the second equation intersects the x-axis.

D. The first equation intersects the x-axis; the second equation does not intersect the x-axis.

Questions 283 -317 are more representative of the difficulty of questions you are likely to encounter.

Question 283:

The vertex of an equilateral triangle is covered by a circle whose radius is half the height of the triangle. What percentage of the triangle is covered by the circle?

A. 12%
B. 16%

C. 23%
D. 33%

E. 41%
F. 50%

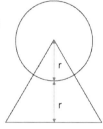

$\frac{1}{2}r^2 \times \frac{\pi}{3} = \frac{\pi}{6}r^2$

Question 284:

Three equal circles fit into a quadrilateral as shown, what is the height of the quadrilateral?

A. $2\sqrt{3}r$
B. $(2+\sqrt{3})r$
C. $(4-\sqrt{3})r$

D. $3r$
E. $4r$
F. More Information Needed

Question 285:

Two pyramids have equal volume and height, one with a square of side length **a** and one with a hexagonal base of side length **b**. What is the ratio of the side length of the bases?

A. $\sqrt{\dfrac{3\sqrt{3}}{2}}$

B. $\sqrt{\dfrac{2\sqrt{3}}{3}}$

C. $\sqrt{\dfrac{3}{2}}$

D. $\dfrac{2\sqrt{3}}{3}$

E. $\dfrac{3\sqrt{3}}{2}$

Question 286:

One 9 cm cube is cut into 3 cm cubes. The total surface area increases by a factor of:

A. $\dfrac{1}{3}$

B. $\sqrt{3}$
C. 3

D. 9
E. 27

Question 287:

A cone has height twice its base width (four times the circle radius). What is the cone angle (half the angle at the vertex)?

A. $30°$

B. $\sin^{-1}\left(\dfrac{r}{2}\right)$

C. $\sin^{-1}\left(\dfrac{1}{\sqrt{17}}\right)$
D. $\cos^{-1}(\sqrt{17})$

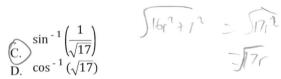

$\sqrt{16r^2 + r^2} = \sqrt{17r^2}$

$= \sqrt{17}r$

Question 288:

A hemispherical speedometer has a maximum speed of 200 mph. What is the angle travelled by the needle at a speed of 70 mph?

$\dfrac{7}{20}\times 180 = 63$

A. $28°$

B. $49°$

C. $63°$

D. $88°$

E. $92°$

Question 289:

Two rhombuses, A and B, are similar. The area of A is 10 times that of B. What is the ratio of the smallest angles over the ratio of the shortest sides?

A. 0

B. $\dfrac{1}{10}$

C. $\dfrac{1}{\sqrt{10}}$

D. $\sqrt{10}$
E. ∞

Question 290:

If $f^{-1}(-x) = \ln(2x^2)$ what is $f(x)$?

A. $\sqrt{\dfrac{e^y}{2}}$
B. $\sqrt{\dfrac{e^{-y}}{2}}$
C. $\dfrac{e^y}{2}$
D. $\dfrac{-e^y}{2}$
E. $\sqrt{\dfrac{e^y}{2}}$

Question 291:

Which of the following is largest for $0 < x < 1$

A. $\log_8(x)$
B. $\log_{10}(x)$
C. e^x
D. x^2
E. $\sin(x)$

Question 292:

x is proportional to y cubed, y is proportional to the square root of z. $x \propto y^3, y \propto \sqrt{z}$.
If z doubles, x changes by a factor of:

A. $\sqrt{2}$
B. 2
C. $2\sqrt{2}$
D. $\sqrt[3]{4}$
E. 4

Question 293:

The area between two concentric circles (shaded) is three times that of the inner circle.

What's the size of the gap?

A. r
B. $\sqrt{2}r$
C. $\sqrt{3}r$
D. $2r$
E. $3r$
F. $4r$

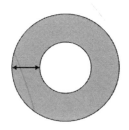

Question 294:

Solve $-x^2 \leq 3x - 4$

A. $x \geq \dfrac{4}{3}$
B. $1 \leq x \leq 4$
C. $x \leq 2$
D. $x \geq 1$ or $x \geq -4$
E. $-1 \leq x \leq \dfrac{3}{4}$

Question 295:

The volume of a sphere is numerically equal to its projected area. What is its radius?

A. $\dfrac{1}{2}$
B. $\dfrac{2}{3}$
C. $\dfrac{3}{4}$
D. $\dfrac{4}{3}$
E. $\dfrac{3}{2}$

Question 296:

What is the range where $x^2 < \dfrac{1}{x}$?

A. $x < 0$
B. $0 < x < 1$
C. $x > 0$
D. $x \geq 1$
E. *None*

Question 297:

Simplify and solve: $(e - a)(e + b)(e - c)(e + d)...(e - z)$?

A. 0
B. e^{26}
C. $e^{26}(a-b+c-d...+z)$
D. $e^{26}(a+b-c+d...-z)$
E. $e^{26}(abcd...z)$
F. None of the above.

Question 298:

Find the value of k such that the vectors $a = -i + 6j$ and $b = 2i + kj$ are perpendicular.

A. -2

B. $-\dfrac{1}{3}$

C. $\dfrac{1}{3}$

D. 2

Question 299:   *A level 이상.*

What is the perpendicular distance between point p with position vector $4i + 5j$ and the line L given by vector equation $r = -3i + j + \lambda(i + 2j)$

A. $2\sqrt{7}$

B. $5\sqrt{2}$

C. $2\sqrt{5}$

D. $7\sqrt{2}$

Question 300:

Find k such that point $\begin{pmatrix} 2 \\ k \\ -7 \end{pmatrix}$ lies within the plane $r = \begin{pmatrix} 2 \\ 3 \\ -1 \end{pmatrix} + \lambda\begin{pmatrix} 4 \\ 1 \\ 0 \end{pmatrix} + \mu\begin{pmatrix} 2 \\ 1 \\ 3 \end{pmatrix}$

A. -2

B. -1

C. 0

D. 1

E. 2

Question 301:   *문제 풀 안됨.*

What is the largest solution to $\sin(-2\theta) = 0.5$ for $\dfrac{\pi}{2} \leq x \leq 2\pi$?

A. $\dfrac{5\pi}{3}$

B. $\dfrac{4\pi}{3}$

C. $\dfrac{5\pi}{6}$

D. $\dfrac{7\pi}{6}$

E. $\dfrac{11\pi}{6}$

Question 302:

$\cos^4(x) - \sin^4(x) \equiv$

A. $\cos(2x)$

B. $2\cos(x)$

C. $\sin(2x)$

D. $sin^{[ro]}(x)cos^{[ro]}(x)$

E. $tan^{[ro]}(x)$

Question 303:

How many real roots does $y = 2x^5 - 3x^4 + x^3 - 4x^2 - 6x + 4$ have?

A. 1

B. 2

C. 3

D. 4

E. 5

$10x^9 - 12x^3 + 7x^2 - 8x - 6$

Question 304:

What is the sum of 8 terms, $\displaystyle\sum_{1}^{8} u_n$, of an arithmetic progression with $u_1 = 2$ and $d = 3$.

A. 15

B. 82

C. 100

D. 184

E. 282

Question 305:

What is the coefficient of the x^2 term in the binomial expansion of $(2 - x)^5$?

A. -80

B. -48

C. 40

D. 48

E. 80

Question 306:   Given you have already thrown a 6, what is the probability of throwing three consecutive 6s using a fair die?

A. $\dfrac{1}{216}$

B. $\dfrac{1}{36}$

C. $\dfrac{1}{6}$

D. $\dfrac{1}{2}$

E. 1

Question 307:

Three people, A, B and C play darts. The probability that they hit a bullseye are respectively $\frac{1}{5}, \frac{1}{4}, \frac{1}{3}$. What is the probability that at least two shots hit the bullseye?

A. $\frac{1}{60}$ B. $\frac{1}{30}$ C. $\frac{1}{12}$ D. $\frac{1}{6}$ E. $\frac{3}{20}$

Question 308:

If probability of having blonde hair is 1 in 4, the probability of having brown eyes is 1 in 2 and the probability of having both is 1 in 8, what is the probability of having neither blonde hair nor brown eyes?

A. $\frac{1}{2}$ B. $\frac{3}{4}$ C. $\frac{3}{8}$ D. $\frac{5}{8}$ E. $\frac{7}{8}$

Question 309:

Differentiate and simplify $y = x(x + 3)^4$

A. $(x + 3)^3$
B. $(x + 3)^4$
C. $x(x + 3)^3$
D. $(5x + 3)(x + 3)^3$
E. $5x^3(x + 3)$

Question 310:

Evaluate $\int_1^2 \frac{2}{x^2} dx$

A. -1 B. $\frac{1}{3}$ C. 1 D. $\frac{21}{4}$ E. 2

Question 311:

Express $\frac{5i}{1 + 2i}$ in the form $a + b i$

A. $1 + 2i$ B. $4i$ C. $1 - 2i$ D. $2 + i$ E. $5 - i$

Question 312:

Simplify $7\log_a(2) - 3\log_a(12) + 5\log_a(3)$

A. $log_{2a}(18)$
B. $log_a(18)$
C. $log_a(7)$
D. $9log_a(17)$
E. $- log_a(7)$

Question 313:

What is the equation of the asymptote of the function $y = \dfrac{2x^2 - x + 3}{x^2 + x - 2}$

A. $x = 0$ B. $x = 2$ C. $y = 0.5$ D. $y = 0$ E. $y = 2$

Question 314:

Find the intersection(s) of the functions $y = e^x - 3$ and $y = 1 - 3e^{-x}$

A. 0 and $\ln (3)$ B. 1 C. $\ln(4)$ and 1 D. $\ln(3)$

Question 315:

Find the radius of the circle $x^2 + y^2 - 6x + 8y - 12 = 0$

A. 3   B. $\sqrt{13}$ C. 5   D. $\sqrt{37}$ E. 12

Question 316:

What value of a minimises $\int_0^a 2\sin(-x)\,dx$?

A. 0.5π B. π C. 2π D. 3π E. 4

Question 317:

When $\dfrac{2x + 3}{(x - 2)(x - 3)^2}$ is expressed as partial fractions, what is the numerator in the $\dfrac{A}{(x - 2)}$ term:

A. -7   B. -1   C. 3   D. 6   E. 7

END OF SECTION

SECTION 2: Writing Task

The Basics

In section 2, you have to write an essay based upon a passage. **There is no choice of essay title** meaning that you have to do the question that comes up. Whilst different questions will inevitably demand differing levels of comprehension and knowledge, it is important to realise that one of the major skills being tested is actually your ability to construct a logical and coherent argument- and to convey it to the lay-reader.

Section 2 of the ECAA is frequently neglected by lots of students, who choose to spend their time on section 1 instead. However, it is possible to rapidly improve in it and given that it may come up at your interview, well worth the time investment!

The aim of section 2 is not to write as much as you can. Rather, the examiner is looking for you to make interesting and well supported points, and tie everything neatly together for a strong conclusion. Make sure you're writing critically and concisely; not rambling on. **Irrelevant material can actually lower your score.**

Essay Structure

Basic Structure

ECAA Essays should follow the standard format of Introduction → Main Body → Conclusion.

The introduction should be the smallest portion of the essay (no more than one small paragraph) and be used to provide a smooth segue into the rather more demanding "argue for/against" part of the question. This main body requires a firm grasp of the concept being discussed and the ability to strengthen and support the argument with a wide variety of examples from multiple fields. This section should give a balanced approach to the question, exploring **at least two distinct ideas**. Supporting evidence should be provided throughout the essay, with examples referred to when possible.

The concluding final part effectively is a chance for you to shine- be brave and make an **innovative yet firmly grounded conclusion** for an exquisite mark. The conclusion should bring together all sides of the argument, in order to reach a clear and concise answer to the question. There should be an obvious logical structure to the essay, which reflects careful planning and preparation.

Paragraphs

Paragraphs are an important formatting tool which show that you have thought through your arguments and are able to structure your ideas clearly. A new paragraph should be used every time a new idea is introduced. There is no single correct way to arrange paragraphs, but it's important that each paragraph flows smoothly from the last. A slick, interconnected essay shows that you have the ability to communicate and organise your ideas effectively.

Remember- the emphasis should remain on quality and not quantity. An essay with fewer paragraphs, but with well-developed ideas, is much more effective than a number of short, unsubstantial paragraphs that fail to fully grasp the question at hand.

Planning

Why should I plan my essay?

The vast **majority of problems are caused by a lack of planning** - usually because students just want to get writing as they are worried about finishing on time. Fourty minutes is long enough to be able to plan your essay well and *still* have time to write it so don't feel pressured to immediately start writing.

There are multiple reasons you should plan your essay for the first 5-10 minutes of section 2:
➢ It allows you to get all your thoughts ready before you put pen to paper.
➢ You'll write faster once you have a plan.
➢ You run the risk of missing the point of the essay or only answering part of it if you don't plan adequately.

How much time should I plan for?

There is no set period of time that should be dedicated to planning, and everyone will dedicate a different length of time to the planning process. You should spend as long planning your essay as you require, but it is essential that you leave enough time to write the essay. As a rough guide, it is **worth spending about 5-10 minutes to plan** and the remaining time on writing the essay. However, this is not a strict rule, and you are advised to tailor your time management to suit your individual style.

How should I go about the planning process?

There are a variety of methods that can be employed in order to plan essays (e.g. bullet-points, mind-maps etc). If you don't already know what works best, it's a good idea to experiment with different methods.

Generally, the first step is to gather ideas relevant to the question, which will form the basic arguments around which the essay is to be built. You can then begin to structure your essay, including the way that points will be linked. At this stage it is worth considering the balance of your argument, and confirming that you have considered arguments from both sides of the debate. Once this general structure has been established, it is useful to consider any examples or real world information that may help to support your arguments. Finally, you can begin to assess the plan as a whole, and establish what your conclusion will be based on your arguments.

Introduction

Why are introductions important?

An introduction provides tutors with their first opportunity to examine your work. The introduction is where first impressions are formed, and these can be extremely important in producing a convincing argument. A well-constructed introduction shows that you have really thought about the question, and can indicate the logical flow of arguments that is to come.

What should an introduction do?

A good introduction should **briefly explain the statement or quote** and give any relevant background information in a concise manner. However, don't fall into the trap of just repeating the statement in a different way. The introduction is the first opportunity to suggest an answer to the question posed- the main body is effectively your justification for this answer.

Main Body

How do I go about making a convincing point?

Each idea that you propose should be supported and justified, in order to build a convincing overall argument. A point can be solidified through a basic Point → Evidence → Evaluation process. By following this process, you can be assured each sentence within a paragraph builds upon the last, and that all the ideas presented are well solidified.

How do I achieve a logical flow between ideas?

One of the most effective ways of displaying a good understanding of the question is to keep a logical flow throughout your essay. This means linking points effectively between paragraphs, and creating a congruent train of thought for the examiner as the argument develops. A good way to generate this flow of ideas is to provide ongoing comparisons of arguments, and discussing whether points support or dispute one another.

Should I use examples?

In short – yes! Examples can help boost the validity of arguments, and can help display high quality writing skills. Examples can add a lot of weight to your argument and make an essay much more relevant to the reader. When using examples, you should ensure that they are relevant to the point being made, as they will not help to support an argument if they are not.

Some questions will provide more opportunities to include examples than others so don't worry if you aren't able to use as many examples as you would have liked. There is no set rule about how many examples should be included!

> ***Top tip!*** Remember that there is no single correct answer to these questions and you're not expected to be able to fit everything onto one page. Instead it's better to pick a few key points to focus on.

Conclusion

The conclusion provides an opportunity to emphasise the **overall sentiment of your essay** which readers can then take away. It should summarise what has been discussed during the main body and give a definitive answer to the question.

Some students use the conclusion to **introduce a new idea that hasn't been discussed**. This can be an interesting addition to an essay, and can help make you stand out. However, it is by no means, a necessity. In fact, a well-organised, 'standard' conclusion is likely to be more effective than an adventurous but poorly executed one.

Common Mistakes

Ignoring the other side of the argument

You need to ensure that you show an appreciation for the fact that there are often two sides to the argument. Where appropriate, you should outline both points of view and how they pertain to the essay's main principles and then come to a reasoned judgement.

A good way to do this is to propose an argument that might be used against you, and then to argue why it doesn't hold true or seem relevant. You may use the format: *"some may say that…but this doesn't seem to be important because…"* in order to dispel opposition arguments, whilst still displaying that you have considered them. For example, *"some may say that fox hunting shouldn't be banned because it is a tradition. However, witch hunting was also once a tradition – we must move on with the times"*.

Missing Topic Sentences

A reader who is pressed for time should be able to read your introduction, the first line of every paragraph and your conclusion and be able to follow your argument. The filling of a paragraph will elaborate your point with examples. But the first sentence of the paragraph should provide the headline point.

> ➤ *Use topic sentences as punchy summaries for the theme of each paragraph*
> ➤ *Include a clear summary of the structure of your essay in your introduction*
> ➤ *Summarize briefly the theme of your points in your conclusion*
> ➤ *Ensure your conclusion also tells the reader your final decision*

Undefined Terms

Debates can be won or lost on the basis of the interpretation of a key term; ensure your interpretation of the key words is clearly explained. For example: "Does science or art shape our world?" Here, your interpretation of what it means to *shape* something is absolutely crucial to lay out before you start writing, so that your reader knows the scope of your argument. If *shape* to you means invent something new (like a potter shaping a pot out of a lump of clay), state this. But if you interpret *shape* to mean a gentle guide or influence on something, state that. You can then be more focused and precise in your discussion. Likewise, for this title ensure you are clear about the scope of what is science and what is art.

> ➤ *Define the key terms within the particular context of the question*
> ➤ *Be clear about your understanding of the scope*

No Sign-Posting

There is a delight to enjoying a long journey if you know (1) where you are going, (2) what you will see on the way and (3) how long it will take to get there. For the reader of your essay, the same logic applies. State briefly but clearly in the final sentence of your introduction the topics you will cover (preferably in the order you will cover them!). You don't need to give the entire game away (don't necessarily tell your reader precisely what your 'wow-factor' will be) but you can give them a solid hint as to your final destination. For example, "Having discussed these arguments in favour and against fox hunting, we conclude with a consideration of the wider issue of the role of governmental institutions in condoning and condemning the traditional pursuits of citizens." It is sometimes tempting to try to surprise your reader with an unexpected twist but this is not best practice for an academic essay.

> ➤ *Don't surprise your reader with unexpected twists in the main essay*
> ➤ *Do be clear in your introduction about the number of points you will make*
> ➤ *Do include your points in the order they will appear*

Long Introductions

Some students can start rambling and make introductions too long and unfocussed. Although background information about the topic can be useful, it is normally not necessary. Instead, the **emphasis should be placed on responding to the question**. Some students also just **rephrase the question** rather than actually explaining it. The examiner knows what the question is, and repeating it in the introduction is simply a waste of space in an essay where you are limited to just one A4 side.

Not including a Conclusion

An essay that lacks a conclusion is incomplete and can signal that the answer has not been considered carefully or that your organisation skills are lacking. **The conclusion should be a distinct paragraph** in its own right and not just a couple of rushed lines at the end of the essay.

Sitting on the Fence

Students sometimes don't reach a clear conclusion. You need to **ensure that you give a decisive answer to the question** and clearly explain how you've reached this judgement. Essays that do not come to a clear conclusion generally have a smaller impact and score lower.

Conclusions with no 'Wow-Factor'

Try to 'zoom out' in your conclusion, rather than merely summarising the points you have made and deciding that one set outweighs the other. Put the question back in a wider context, so that your decision has a wow-factor for why it really matters. For instance, if you have answered the question, "Is world peace achievable?" and you think it isn't, say why this matters. For example: "In an age of nuclear capability, attempts to achieve the impossible is a waste of scarce resources, so we'd be better off focusing policy and diplomacy on building safety nets to prevent escalations of inevitable conflicts into another world war."

> ➤ *Don't only repeat your arguments again in your conclusion*
> ➤ *Don't sit on the fence in your conclusion*
> ➤ *Do use the conclusion to zoom out for the final punchline: why does this matter?*

Missing the Point

Ensure you have identified what you think the 'Turning Point' of the question is, before you start writing. Within the title, which may be long and literary, identify the single core issue for you that you will discuss. For example, with the question, "Has the "digital age" destroyed the human right to anonymity?", restate it as a simple statement: the key question is whether previous to the introduction of digital technology we had a human right to anonymity which has now disappeared. You can then anchor your argument clearly on whether such a right had always existed before (perhaps so, perhaps not) and whether it has now disappeared (if it ever existed). By restating the key question, you will auto-generate a clear structure for yourself to follow.

> ➤ *Work out the hinge of the question before you start writing and state it clearly*

Worked Essay Questions

Passage 1

In 1972, the teenage king of Bhutan, Jigme Singye Wangchuck, declared that "gross national happiness is more important than gross domestic product". The sound bite has been echoed approvingly down the years, although the king may just have been making excuses. Bhutanese GDP per person was then the grinding poverty of about a dollar a day. If I were king of such a country, I'd be tempted to change the subject, too.

Clearly he had a point. Most of us would rather be poor and happy than rich and depressed. If so, gross national happiness seems a fine goal. But it is one thing for a monarch to announce that happiness is important. It's quite another to make people happy. Shangri-La does not move from fiction to reality just because we desire it.

Bhutan has not always lived up to its own hype. Same-sex intercourse is illegal, which suggests a country with a less-than-expansive view of whose happiness matters. Three decades ago, around 100,000 of the Nepali-speaking Lhotshampa minority fled Bhutan to escape military persecution during a campaign of ethnic cleansing on a colossal scale. One-sixth of the entire population of Bhutan ended up in refugee camps in Nepal.

Even setting aside this enormity, it's hard to see that Bhutan paid much more than lip service to gross national happiness. They hosted conferences, but according to a recent IMF working paper, nobody in the government collected systematic indicators on happiness until 2005. The World Happiness Report ranks Bhutan at 97th out of 156 countries, down from 84th a few years ago. Happiness is easy to venerate, but hard to generate, and even harder to measure.

Consider some of the issues that are notoriously bypassed by GDP, the most common measure of economic activity: digital services are hard to value, while by design GDP omits any consideration of inequality or environmental damage. Unpaid work — of which men do a great deal, and women a great deal more — is also left out.

But if our aim is (for example) to reduce carbon emissions, we don't achieve it by moaning about GDP. We achieve it with specific policies such as carbon taxes and investments in public transport and a renewable-friendly electric grid. Neither gender equality nor respect for unpaid work would be automatically improved by any change in the way national income accounts are computed.

The specifics matter when it comes to happiness, too. Broad research into the causes of national happiness has tended to produce banal conclusions: we tend to compare ourselves to others, unemployment makes us miserable, and we hate being ill. There is nothing here to suggest that we need to overhaul commonplace policies such as redistributive taxation, the avoidance of recessions, and support for public health.

Just as with GDP itself, it is only when we move to the specifics that gross national happiness becomes useful. Richard Layard, one of the leading happiness researchers, argues that mental illness is a leading cause of misery, and that it can be treated very cost-effectively. That seems useful enough to me, but that doesn't seem to require economists' focus to realise.

QUESTION
"Economists should be more concerned with happiness and wellbeing than GDP."
Discuss with reference to the passage above.

Example Plan

Introduction: Set the scene...

- Define "concerned with". This could mean "focus on..." or "worried about". Here I take it here to mean a that latter because it allows for a more expansive essay, however either would be appropriate given context.
- The key question to be answered is therefore: Should economic analysis and policies be focussed on improving a nation's happiness, instead of conventional measures of wealth and prosperity?

Paragraph 1: Just because it's better doesn't make it the focus...

- Traditionally economic analysis and economic policies have been focussed on promoting economic growth conventionally measured through GDP per capita. The article makes the assertion that "many of us would rather be poor and happy, than rich and miserable".
- On this logic, economists and the policies they devise to help governments, should be focussed on generating happiness for people rather than wealth.
- Yet this assumes that economists and their policies should be focussed on outcomes that are most desirable, without paying attention to pragmatics.

Paragraph 2: Challenge 1 – It isn't pragmatic to be concerned with happiness...

- One reason for economists remaining focussed on GDP is that it isn't pragmatic to be focussed on the alternative; namely happiness and wellbeing.
- Happiness is notoriously hard to measure. As the article explains generic measures of happiness are subject to the same criticisms as GDP (see paragraph 7 in the article).
- Equally it is not clear that happiness is the same for every person. Whilst wealth is somewhat consistent across individuals e.g. more money and better-quality stuff = more wealth; it is not clear that what makes me happy makes any other individual happy. In a world where policy is general and impacts all, economists cannot aim to please everyone.

Paragraph 3: It isn't right to be concerned with happiness...

- This all assumes thus far that happiness is what economists **should** be concerned about if only it were possible to measure and practical to increase.
- However, GDP has a lot going for it, indeed it has remained the headline measure for the IMF even for Bhutan for much of the last few decades (paragraph 4).
- The criticism of GDP in paragraph 5, makes a compelling case against it's general nature, but whilst it advocates for measuring specifics, it does not say that national income (GDP) is the wrong measure entirely.
- Indeed, measuring wealth/national income is crucially important – without it public services cannot be provided, a country struggles to trade for things it needs and it's people have limited access to resources, capital or goods that are required for living a reasonable quality of life.
- There is therefore a compelling argument for national income/GDP to remain the concern of economists for both analysis and policy purposes.

Conclusion

- Summarize the points:
  - The article seems to suggest at points that happiness should be the concern of economists, above GDP and that it should be considered with specificity to be useful to economists.
- Having decided in this plan to argue against the statement summarise your three points:
  - Take the assertion that happiness is more important than GDP to be right however this isn't enough to suggest that it should be the primary concern of economists.
  - It isn't pragmatic to be concerned with happiness and therefore it shouldn't be the primary concern
  - It isn't even right to be concerned with happiness anyway.

Zoom out and say why the question really matters and conclude.

Passage 2

THE annual labour of every nation is the fund which originally supplies it with all the necessaries and conveniences of life which it annually consumes, and which consist always either in the immediate produce of that labour, or in what is purchased with that produce from other nations.

According therefore as this produce, or what is purchased with it, bears a greater or smaller proportion to the number of those who are to consume it, the nation will be better or worse supplied with all the necessaries and conveniences for which it has occasion.

But this proportion must in every nation be regulated by two different circumstances; first, by the skill, dexterity, and judgment with which its labour is generally applied; and, secondly, by the proportion between the number of those who are employed in useful labour, and that of those who are not so employed. Whatever be the soil, climate, or extent of territory of any nation, the abundance or scantiness of its annual supply must, in that particular situation, depend upon those two circumstances.

The abundance or scantiness of this supply, too, seems to depend more upon the former of those two circumstances than upon the latter. Among the savage nations of hunters and fishers, every individual who is able to work, is more or less employed in useful labour, and endeavours to provide, as well as he can, the necessaries and conveniences of life, for himself, or such of his family or tribe as are either too old, or too young, or too infirm to go a hunting and fishing. Such nations, however, are so miserably poor that, from mere want, they are frequently reduced, or, at least, think themselves reduced, to the necessity sometimes of directly destroying, and sometimes of abandoning their infants, their old people, and those afflicted with lingering diseases, to perish with hunger, or to be devoured by wild beasts. Among civilised and thriving nations, on the contrary, though a great number of people do not labour at all, many of whom consume the produce of ten times, frequently of a hundred times more labour than the greater part of those who work; yet the produce of the whole labour of the society is so great that all are often abundantly supplied, and a workman, even of the lowest and poorest order, if he is frugal and industrious, may enjoy a greater share of the necessaries and conveniences of life than it is possible for any savage to acquire

(Adam Smith, Wealth of Nations)

QUESTION
"What is Adam Smith argument in the passage. Do you agree or disagree? (Use examples from modern economics)
Discuss with reference to the passage above.

Example Plan

Introduction: What is Adam Smith's Argument in the passage?

- Smith's argument can essentially be deconstructed as follows:
  - Refer first to Para 3 where he explains that the proportion that is produced in a country versus the population (GDP per capita) will be determined by the application of labour and the number of people employed. This goes against an argument that soil, climate, geography of the nation can influence the economic wealth of that country.
  - Smith then goes on to claim in paragraph 4 that wealth in fact whilst dependent on both factors, depends on the former of the two more than the latter; that production is about skill not number of worker. He claims nations that are poor are often at full employment but do not work with skill. In a wealthy society however, it is often the case that individuals are not all employed, but the production of a few well employed is so great to as provide for all.

Paragraph 1: Adam Smith's logic does seem to apply to modern countries?

- Smith is arguing that the reason countries have become wealthy is because they apply labour with more precision, and have more skilled labour.
- Take the cadre of modern day developed economies: they are not the most populous countries in the world e.g. UK, Japan, European countries are all some of the most developed. They do however all have developed industries (service orientated or high-skilled manufacturing economies with highly skilled labour forces). Additionally, they do also have higher rates of unemployment.
- This all seems to validate Smith's argument that it matters not the rate of employment but rather the skill of the employed that drive economic prosperity.
- Expand with examples of your own e.g. UK development in 80s and 90s, rise of Japan and the Far-East as skilled labour economies for hi-tech manufacturing (Sony, Samsung etc...)

Paragraph 2: Employing lots of people hasn't seemed to drive wealth.

- Adam Smith make's a coherent argument for population size and even employment rates not being a significant contributing factor to the wealth of a nation. In fact, he suggests that you have historically seen many societies where all employable individual's (health and age dependent) work but are savage and primitive.
- Whilst extreme, there is validation for Adam Smith's logic in modern day examples. Possible examples include Asian economies where numerous individuals (young, old, infirm and those who can work) are employed in low wage jobs such as sweat shops etc... other examples could be rural economies in Africa.
- The economies whilst at full employment do not reap the rewards of their labour, the lack of high skilled individuals to develop high value products means that the majority of the valuable assets are owned or traded   overseas.

Paragraph 3: However, Adam Smith ignores key factors that influence growth in a globalised world.

- Some could argue that Adam Smith's argument no longer applies in today's globalised world.
- Today when economies are integrated it could be no longer argued that wealth need be driven by internal processes, instead the ways in which a country is linked with, and to whom, can be said to drive growth and wealth.
- Take for example some of the countries in Africa where it is shown that post-colonial connections to their former colonial power, are correlated with wealth because of trade links. This has nothing to do with labour etc...

Conclusion

- Summarize the points:
    - Adam Smith's argument does seem to reflect the economic facts we see in the modern world.
        - This applies in terms of the precise application of skilled labour
        - It also appears to apply in the idea that large populations and close to full employment does not drive economic wealth.
- Zoom out and say why the question really matters (give your essay the 'wow-factor'):
    - Important to understand for policy decisions in terms of driving economic growth: to drive a wealthy economy policy should focus on training and skills development, rather than getting everyone to full employment. However, it should be noted that this relies on strong redistribution as wealth can then become concentrated.

Passage 3 – Animal Spirits

Even apart from the instability due to speculation, there is the instability due to the characteristic of human nature that a large proportion of our positive activities depend on spontaneous optimism rather than on a mathematical expectation, whether moral or hedonistic or economic. Most, probably, of our decisions to do something positive, the full consequences of which will be drawn out over many days to come, can only be taken as a result of animal spirits—of a spontaneous urge to action rather than inaction, and not as the outcome of a weighted average of quantitative benefits multiplied by quantitative probabilities. Enterprise only pretends to itself to be mainly actuated by the statements in its own prospectus, however candid and sincere. Only a little more than an expedition to the South Pole, is it based on an exact calculation of benefits to come. Thus if the animal spirits are dimmed and the spontaneous optimism falters, leaving us to depend on nothing but a mathematical expectation, enterprise will fade and die; —though fears of loss may have a basis no more reasonable than hopes of profit had before.

It is safe to say that enterprise which depends on hopes stretching into the future benefits the community as a whole. But individual initiative will only be adequate when reasonable calculation is supplemented and supported by animal spirits, so that the thought of ultimate loss which often overtakes pioneers, as experience undoubtedly tells us and them, is put aside as a healthy man puts aside the expectation of death.

This means, unfortunately, not only that slumps and depressions are exaggerated in degree, but that economic prosperity is excessively dependent on a political and social atmosphere which is congenial to the average business man.

(John Maynard Keynes)

QUESTION
What does Keynes mean by "Animal Spirits"? What are the implications, if true, for current economic policy? (Discuss with examples).

Example Plan

Introduction:
- Animal Spirits according to Keynes are the "spontaneous urge to action rather than inaction, and not as the outcome of a weighted average of quantitative benefits multiplied by quantitative probabilities".
- By this Keynes means that despite the economic assumption of rationality, a great deal of decision making is dependent upon unexplained or spontaneous feelings by humans; those animal spirits that exist within us all.
- Keynes sees animal spirits as that part of us all that emotionally drives our decision making either by instilling confidence or fear and as such, "economic prosperity is excessively dependent the political and social atmosphere".

Paragraph 1: Implication for economic policy 1 – Policy based on assumptions of rationality can sometimes not have the desired impact

- One of the major implications for economic policy of animal spirits is that when economic policy is implemented then the consequences are often unpredictable.
- For example: at this point you could use any example but below is an example
- Expansionary Fiscal policy: e.g. monetary spending or tax cuts/breaks. The intention of this policy is to increase disposable income with the intention of increasing consumption and investment, yielding economic growth. However, animal spirits suggest that whilst theoretically, a rational individual would act in accordance with a rational analysis of the benefits from spending increases, in fact their propensity to spend is highly dependent on animal spirits in the form of confidence, trust and other emotions that could induce spending decisions.
- This would then lead into the next implication – that governments should try and influence animal spirits.

Paragraph 2: Implication for policy 2 – Policy should sometimes aim to impact animal spirits

- To ensure the effectiveness of economic policies enacted by governments, they should sometimes try to impact animal spirits, or at least not neglect them.
- Why? The government cannot neglect animal spirits because they are so influential. Therefore, in making decisions around policy the government should consider the impact they can have on these sentiments e.g. confidence, trust etc…
- Examples for this could include scheduling of events such as forecasts and economic announcements, central bank messaging, statements to the media, geo-political events and their handling, elections, wars and other national social events.

Paragraph 3: Implication for policy 3 – Recessions can be unpredictable

- Another major implication stemming from the concept of animal spirits, is its consequences for the unpredictable nature of certain events.
- For example, stories of corruption and broken trust can reduce confidence, and that can greatly contribute to economic depressions and confidence being undermined can lead to crisis. Possible examples include:
  - Stories – humans get behind stories and can be positive. E.g. is story of the internet and a new era of tech fuelled one of history's biggest stock market bubbles in the early 2000s. Similarly, during the depression in the US in the 1890s the run on the banks was caused by stories spread of corruption and fragility in the financial system, when in fact many were untrue.
  - In the 1980s crisis ensued when moral hazard undermined confidence; savings and loan entrepreneurs made risky investments knowing that the government would rescue them – similar example in 2008 Sub-Prime Mortgage crisis. Erosion of confidence from this in some cases sparked and certainly deepened the recessions.
- This is worrying for policy makers because it seems to imply that there are some factors that are simply out of their control. (At this point you could introduce an argument in defence of policy makers which suggests that since they cannot control animal spirits perhaps they need to be wholly reactive etc…).

Conclusion:

- Summarize the points:
  - Animal Spirits can distort the theoretically predicted impact of economic policies which are based on the assumptions of rationality
  - A second implication for policy makers is that they should sometime not only account for, but aim to influence animal spirits using communications or timings of events.
  - A third implication of animal spirits is that they render economic events such as recessions somewhat unpredictable.
- Likely conclusion is that clearly animal spirits hold great implications of economic policy makers in a variety of ways; including potentially very negative and therefore cannot be ignored and must be accounted for as much as possible.

Passage 4

Most institutions in the country are businesses – shops, factories, energy companies, airlines, and train companies, to name a few types. They are the bedrock of society, employ most people in it and it is, thus, crucial that we examine their values.

The overriding objective of businesses is to make the most profit (i.e. maximise on revenue and minimise on costs). The notion was first popularly expounded by Adam Smith in his book, 'The Wealth of Nations' in 1776. Furthermore, his view was that if an individual considers merely their own interests to create and sell goods or services for the most profit, the invisible hand of the market will lead that activity to maximise the welfare of society. For example, in order to maximise profits, sellers will only produce and sell goods that society wants. If they try to sell things people don't want, no one would buy it. This is how the free market works. Indeed, the focus on profit is the basis on which companies operate and encourages them to innovate and produce goods that consumers want, such as iPhones and computers. So there are clear benefits to the profit maximisation theory.

This is a more effective society than, for example, a communist society where the government decides what to produce – as the government has no accurate way of deciding what consumers need and want. Arguably, the poverty that communist regimes such as the Soviet Union created have instilled this notion further.

However, were companies left to their own devices to engage in profit maximisation, what would stop them from exploiting workers? What would stop them from dumping toxic chemicals into public rivers? Engaging in such practices would reduce their costs of production, which would increase their profits. However, this would be very damaging to the environment. Accordingly, other objectives should be relevant. Businesses can also do other bad things to make a profit as well. For example, selling products to people who don't want or need them.

Corporate social responsibility entails other possible objectives for businesses, such as a consideration of the interests of stakeholders. A stakeholder is, in essence, anyone who is significantly affected by a company decision, such as employees or the local community. One business decision can have huge impacts on stakeholders. For example, a decision to transfer a call centre from the UK to India would likely increase profits, as wage costs for Indian workers can be much lower than that of British workers. This increase in profits would benefit the shareholders, however, it negatively harms other stakeholders. It would make many employees redundant. Here, there is arguably a direct conflict between profit maximisation and employees' interest. Nonetheless, moving call centres abroad does not always work. Given the different cultures and accents, companies have received complaints from frustrated customers. This, in fact, led BT to bring back a number of call centres to the UK.

However, the objective of profit maximisation has not always led to maximum welfare for society. Arguably, as banks sought to maximise their profits, they lent money to individuals who could not afford to pay it back. Eventually, many borrowers stopped meeting their repayments and lost banks enormous amounts. This led to a need for banks to be bailed out by the government and Lehman Brothers; one of the largest US banks that collapsed. Arguably, though, this was more due to idiocy rather than profit maximisation alone – in the end, the banks lost billions.

QUESTION
"Enforcing Corporate Social Responsibility interferes with the market's ability to give people what they want." Discuss with reference to the passage above.

Example Plan

Introduction:

- Define Corporate Social Responsibility (from the passage). The market: here, we mean the goods and services offered for sale by businesses and bought by consumers. People: here we mean both the consumers in the market and those not participating in the market.
- The key question: If businesses are driven by the objective to maximise profits, does the market truly give people what they want?

Paragraph 1:

- Adam Smith's invisible hand tells us that the market will allocate resources to maximise the welfare of society. If goods were produced and not demanded, this would waste resources. This cannot happen as the resources used to make these goods would be allocated to make other, demanded, goods.
- *Passage Example:* "Sellers will only produce and sell goods that society wants." The businesses may be maximising profits, but they can only do so within the constraints of selling items that are wanted by the people. Thus, what is on offer in a market is determined by the people's wants.

Paragraph 2:

- We need Corporate Social Responsibility to prevent the profit maximisation of businesses affecting stakeholders who are not necessarily the direct consumer of the good or service being produced. Their loss may outweigh the gains of those engaged in the transaction and so we have a net loss,
- *Passage Example*: "Corporate social responsibility entails other possible objectives for businesses, such as consideration of the interests of stakeholders."

Paragraph 3:

- The problem here is not the functioning of the market, but instead all the people not fully understanding the impact of their consumption: with full information, people's wants will be satisfied by the market,
- *Passage Example:* "Dumping toxic chemicals into public rivers... would be very damaging to the environment." If the pollution is common knowledge, and if the majority of people think it is bad, they will buy goods from an alternative green business, and the polluting company will go out of business.
- *Passage Example:* "A decision to transfer a call centre from the UK to India ... would make many employees redundant." If this is common knowledge the majority will switch their consumption to another business; indeed, we see BT had to relocate back to the UK to re-cooperate customers.

Paragraph 4:

- It may not be possible to fully inform customers, in which case the argument for regulation enforcing business responsibility is clear: external referees are needed to identify the good which is preferred for people and ensure they get the right one in the market.
- *Passage Example*: "Many borrowers stopped meeting their repayments..." Borrowers bought loans that were not fully understood by the players in the market and were too risky.

Conclusion

- Summarize the points:
    - Allocation is determined by people's demand: any interferences undermine people's wants.
    - Allocations may affect other stakeholders resulting in net-loss of welfare.
    - If all stakeholders (consumers, businesses and externally affected people) understand all the repercussions of production, wants will be satisfied directly in the market.
    - Full information for everyone is not feasible in some contexts.
- Now decide for yourself one way or another…
- Zoom out and say why the question really matters (just pick one to give your essay the 'wow-factor'):
    - Government Intervention is needed to ensure market interactions are net-beneficial to society, not just to the active buyers and sellers. CSR gives a voice to the wants of the silent victims of markets.

Passage 5

"What are the rules which men naturally observe in exchanging them [goods] for money or for one another, I shall now proceed to examine. These rules determine what may be called the relative or exchangeable value of goods. The word 'Value', it is to be observed, has two different meanings, and sometimes expresses the utility of some particular object, and sometimes the power of purchasing other goods which the possession of that object conveys. The one may be called "value in use;" the other, "value in exchange." The things which have the greatest value in use have frequently little or no value in exchange; on the contrary, those which have the greatest value in exchange have frequently little or no value in use. Nothing is more useful than water: but it will purchase scarcely anything; scarcely anything can be had in exchange for it. A diamond, on the contrary, has scarcely any use-value; but a very great quantity of other goods may frequently be had in exchange for it."

(Adam Smith, Wealth of Nations)

This passage articulates a paradox in economics knows as the Paradox of Value or Diamond-Water Paradox. Smith noted that, even though life cannot exist without water and can easily exist without diamonds, diamonds are, pound for pound, vastly more valuable than water.

In a further passage Smith explains: "The real price of every thing, what every thing really costs to the man who wants to acquire it, is the toil and trouble of acquiring it."
(Adam Smith, Wealth of Nations)

Thus, Smith's explanation was the labour theory of value. This theory stated that the price of a good reflected the amount of labour and resources required to bring it to market. Smith believed diamonds were more expensive than water because they were more difficult to bring to market. Price on this view was related to a factor of production (namely, labour) and not to the point of view of the consumer (in which case there would be a relationship between price and utility.

QUESTION
How convincing is Smith's explanation of Labour Theory of Value as a resolution of the 'Diamond-Water Paradox'? What other explanations are there, and are they more convincing?

Example Plan

Introduction:
- Introduce and summarize Smith's problem: simply that despite their differing values to humans, with water being integral to life and diamonds a superficial luxury diamonds hold far more value.
- Smith explains this by suggesting that the reason for this is because the value of a good is related to the labour involved in it production.
- State the structure of the essay and you likely conclusion since this is an argumentative piece.

Paragraph 1: The Labour Theory of Value

- Start by assessing the Labour Theory of Value as a convincing argument for resolving the Diamond-Water Paradox.
- On the one hand this seems logical because products which take a lot of skill to produce, or a lot of time will often cost more. E.g. for something with high production costs (directly related to the labour) such as an iPhone which must be designed, produced and shipped.
- However, labour theory of value struggles when trying to explain the price attached to good which have little or no production process or value. For example consider a perfectly formed gemstone found on a path, which would not have a lower market price than one which is produced artificially through significant labour or even one which has been mined and cut and polished through hard work.

Paragraph 2: Subjective Value – the opposite of Labour Theory seems more likely

- Another argument against the validity of the Labour theory of value is that it is not the case that costs and labour drive price, in fact price drives labour and cost.
- Consider goods that have high value such as fine wine, which is not valuable because it derives from expensive land and is produced by highly paid workers who exert effort. In fact, the price seems more likely to be the driver of the costs, because the product is valuable, the means of production are valuable.
- This suggests that the value of a product lies in the value people attach to it; so for a solution to this paradox we must look to why people value diamonds more than water.

Paragraph 3: Alternative 1 – Scarcity: Supply and Demand

- One clear alternative way of solving the argument lies in the relative rarity of the products then.
- Diamonds are rarer and therefore utility from a single diamond, is more valuable demand outstrips supply by a greater amount, than with water which is in abundant supply, thereby driving the price up.
- This is simple demand and supply, but can be countered by the following logic: Whilst it is true that supply of diamonds is much lower, it is not clear why demand would be the same. Indeed, it seems likely that demand for water is much higher than that of diamonds, water is more essential for life and has more uses.

Paragraph 4: Alternative 2 – Scarcity: marginal Utility

- The alternative means of solving this paradox lie in the theory of marginal utility; which suggests that the price of a good is derived from its most important use – namely that the price is determined by the usefulness of each unit of a good not the total utility of a good.
- Since diamonds are rarer, it is likely that they are put to their most important use thereby holding greater value. Since water is so abundant, each additional unit of water that becomes available can be applied to less urgent uses as more urgent uses for water are satisfied.
- Under this logic, any unit of water becomes less valuable because it is put to less and less valuable use. Conversely each unit of diamond is more valuable because it is in less supply so put to more use. One additional diamond is worth more than one additional glass of water for example.
- A further example for this logic comes from considering a man in a desert who would have greater marginal use for water than for diamonds, so water would hold more value for him, due to scarcity.

Conclusion

- Summarize the points:
  - Adam Smith solves the paradox with the labour theory of value
  - There is an opposite argument: subjective theory of value which yields two alternatives
  - Supply and Demand simply drives the higher price
  - The answer lies in the different marginal utilities of the goods due to their scarcity
- Give your answer as to which is more convincing backing it up with either logical reasoning or persuasive examples.
- Zoom out and say why this is important – fundamentally important question about value of goods and services. Important to consider how prices of these essential, yet currently abundant goods, may change as they become more scarce e.g. fossil fuels, clean water etc…

Intro
Does it explain or just repeat?
Does it set up the main body?
Does it get to the point?

Main Body
Are enough points being made? *[Breadth]*
Are the points explained sufficiently? *[Depth]*
Does the argument make sense? *[Strength]*

Conclusion
Does it follow naturally from the main body?
Does it consider both sides of the argument?
Does it answer the original question?

Final Advice

✓ Always answer the question clearly – this is the key thing examiner look for in an essay.

✓ Analyse each argument made, justifying or dismissing with logical reasoning.

✓ Keep an eye on the time/space available – an incomplete essay may be taken as a sign of a candidate with poor organisational skills.

✓ Ensure each paragraph has a new theme that is clearly differentiated from the previous one (don't just use a new paragraph to break your text up)

✓ Leave yourself time to write a conclusion – however short – that tells your reader which side of the fence you're on

✓ Do plan your essay before you start writing even the introduction; don't be tempted to dive straight into it

✓ Use pre-existing knowledge when possible – examples and real world data can be a great way to strengthen an argument- but don't make up statistics!

✓ Present ideas in a neat, logical fashion (easier for an examiner to absorb).

✓ Complete some practice questions in advance, in order to best establish your personal approach to the paper (particularly timings, how you plan etc.).

✗ Attempt to answer a question that you don't fully understand, or ignore part of a question.

✗ Rush or attempt to use too many arguments – it is much better to have fewer, more substantial points.

✗ Attempt to be too clever, or present false knowledge to support an argument – a tutor may call out incorrect facts etc.

✗ Panic if you don't know the answer the examiner wants – there is no right answer, the essay is not a test of knowledge but a chance to display reasoning skill. Start by defining the words in the question to get your mind thinking about ways to approach it

✗ Leave an essay unfinished – if time/space is short, wrap up the essay early in order to provide a conclusive response to the question. If you've only got a couple of minutes left, summarize your remaining points in a short bullet point each; these bullets contain just the topic sentence and (optionally) a quote from the passage to illustrate your point

ANSWERS

Answer Key

Q	A	Q	A	Q	A	Q	A	Q	A	Q	A	Q	A
1	B	51	A	101	C	151	C	201	D & E	251	A	301	E
2	E	52	C & E	102	A	152	B	202	C	252	C	302	A
3	E	53	D	103	B	153	E	203	C	253	C	303	C
4	D	54	D	104	B	154	C	204	C	254	C	304	C
5	E	55	B	105	E	155	B	205	C	255	B	305	E
6	E	56	D	106	E	156	E	206	D	256	D	306	A
7	A	57	A	107	C	157	D	207	C	257	E	307	D
8	C	58	B	108	B	158	C	208	B	258	D	308	C
9	D	59	C	109	C	159	B	209	C	259	D	309	D
10	C	60	B	110	D	160	C	210	C	260	B	310	A
11	E & F	61	C	111	C	161	D	211	C	261	E	311	D
12	D	62	D	112	B	162	A	212	E	262	E	312	B
13	C	63	D	113	D	163	D	213	A	263	B	313	E
14	B	64	C	114	C	164	B	214	C	264	C	314	A
15	A	65	C	115	C	165	D	215	E	265	A	315	D
16	C	66	C	116	A	166	D	216	E	266	C	316	C
17	B	67	A	117	C	167	C	217	C	267	B	317	E
18	C	68	C	118	B	168	C	218	E	268	B		
19	D	69	A	119	E	169	C	219	E	269	B		
20	B & C	70	E	120	D	170	A	220	E	270	C		
21	B	71	C	121	C	171	B	221	B	271	C		
22	B & D	72	B	122	B	172	D	222	C	272	A		
23	D	73	B	123	E	173	B	223	B	273	C		
24	F	74	C	124	C	174	A	224	B	274	D		
25	D	75	B	125	C	175	D	225	C	275	C		

#	Ans	#	Ans	#	Ans	#	Ans	#	Ans	#	Ans
26	D	76	C	126	E	176	B	226	D	276	D
27	B & D	77	E	127	B	177	C	227	C	277	A
28	B	78	D	128	D	178	B	228	B	278	C
29	C	79	C	129	C	179	D	229	A	279	B
30	C	80	B	130	D	180	F	230	F	280	B
31	D	81	E	131	E	181	C	231	D	281	A
32	B	82	D	132	B	182	B	232	A	282	C
33	C	83	A	133	C	183	A	233	B	283	C
34	B	84	C	134	C	184	B	234	A	284	B
35	E	85	A	135	D	185	A	235	F	285	A
36	B	86	B	136	B	186	C	236	D	286	C
37	D	87	C	137	E	187	C	237	A	287	E
38	D	88	A	138	C	188	C	238	D	288	C
39	C	89	B	139	A	189	C	239	D	289	C
40	C	90	F	140	C	190	C	240	F	290	E
41	B	91	C	141	C	191	D	241	B	291	C
42	C	92	E	142	D	192	C	242	C	292	C
43	C	93	B	143	A	193	D	243	B	293	A
44	C	94	B	144	D	194	C	244	C	294	D
45	D	95	C	145	D	195	C	245	A	295	C
46	C	96	C	146	C	196	C	246	A	296	B
47	E	97	C	147	C	197	C	247	C	297	A
48	D	98	F	148	C	198	E	248	B	298	C
49	C	99	C	149	E	199	C	249	D	299	C
50	A	100	A	150	D	200	C	250	C	300	E

Worked Answers

Question 1: B

By making a grid and filling in the relevant information the days Dr James works can be deduced:

	Sunday	Monday	Tuesday	Wednesday	Thursday	Friday	Saturday
Dr Evans	X	√	X	X	√	√	√
Dr James	X	√	√	√	√	X	√
Dr Luca	X	X	√	√	X	√	√

➢ No one works Sunday.
➢ All work Saturday.
➢ Dr Evans works Mondays and Fridays.
➢ Dr Luca cannot work Monday or Thursday.
➢ So, Dr James works Monday.
➢ And, Dr Evans and Dr James must work Thursday.
➢ Dr Evans cannot work 4 days consecutively so he cannot work Wednesday.
➢ Which means Dr James and Luca must work Wednesday.
➢ (mentioned earlier in the question) Dr Evans only works 4 days, so cannot work Tuesday.
➢ Which means Dr James and Luca work Tuesday.
➢ Dr James cannot work 5 days consecutively so cannot work Friday.
➢ Which means Dr Luca must work Friday.

Question 2: E

Working algebraically, using the call out rate as C, and rate per mile as M.
So,   C + 4m = 11
C + 5m = 13
Hence; (C + 5m) – (C + 4m) = £13 - £11
M = £2
Substituting this back into C + 4m = 11
C + (4 x 2) = 11
Hence, C = £3
Thus a ride of 9 mile will cost £3 + (9 x £2) = £21.

Question 3: E

Use the information to create a Venn diagram.
We don't know the exact position of both Trolls and Elves, so **A** and **D** are true. Goblins are mythical but not magical, so **C** is true. Gnomes are neither so **B** is true. But **E** is not true.

Question 4: D

The best method may be work backwards from 7pm. The packing (15 minutes) of all 100 tiles must have started by 6:45pm, hence the cooling (20 minutes) of the last 50 tiles started by 6:25pm, and the heating (45 minutes) by 5:40pm. The first 50 heating (45 minutes) must have started by 4:35pm, and cooling (20 minutes) by 5:20pm. The decoration (50 minutes) of the second 50 can occur anytime during 4:35pm- 5:40pm as this is when the first 50 are heating and cooling in the kiln, and so does not add time. The first 50 take 50 minutes to decorate and so must be started by 3:45pm.

Question 5: E

Speed = distance/time. Hence for the faster, pain impulse the speed is 1m/ 0.001 seconds. Hence the speed of the pain impulse is 1000 metres per second. The normal touch impulse is half this speed and so is 500 metres per second.

Question 6: E

Using the months of the year, Melissa could be born in March or May, Jack in June or July and Alina in April or August. With the information that Melissa and Jack's birthdays are 3 months apart the only possible combination is March and June. Hence Alina must be born in August, which means it is another 7 months until Melissa's birthday in March.

Question 7: A

PC Bryan cannot work with PC Adams because they have already worked together for 7 days in a row, so **C** is incorrect. **B** is incorrect because if PC Dirk worked with PC Bryan that would leave PC Adams with PC Carter who does not want to work with him. PC Carter can work with PC Bryan.

Question 8: C

Paying for my next 5 appointments will cost £50 per appointment before accounting for the 10% reduction, hence the cost counting the deduction is £45 per appointment. So the total for 4 appointments = 5 x £45 = £225 for the hair. Then add £15 for the first manicure and £10 x 2 for the subsequent manicures using the same bottle of polish bringing an overall total of £260.

Question 9: D

Elena is married to Alex or David, but we are told that Bertha is married to David and so Alex must be married to Elena. Hence David, Bertha, Elena and Alex are the four adults. Bertha and David's child is Gemma. So Charlie and Frankie must be Alex and Elena's two children. Leaving only options **A** or **D** as possibilities. Only Frankie and Gemma are girls so Charlie must be a boy.

Question 10: C

Using, x (minutes) as the, unknown amount of time, the second student took to examine, we can plot the time taken with the information provided thus:

	1st student		2nd student		3rd student
1st examination:	4x	1	2x	1	2x
		Break: 8 minutes			
1st examination:	x	1	x	1	x

 Hence the total time taken, 45minutes (14:30-15:15)
Is represented by, $4x + 2x + 2x + x + x + x + 1 + 1 + 8 + 1 + 1$
$$45 \text{ minutes} = 11x \text{ (minutes)} + 12 \text{ minutes}$$
$$33 \text{ minutes} = 11x \text{ (minutes)}$$
Hence, x = 3 minutes, so the amount of time the second student took the first time, 2x, is 6 minutes.

Question 11: E & F

To work out the amount of change is the sum £5 - (2 x £1.65), which = £3.30. Logically we can then work out that the 3 coins in the change that are the same must be 1p as no other 3 coin combination can yield £1.70 when made up with 5 more coins. Thus we know that 3 of the coins are 1p, 1p & 1p. We can then deduce that there must also have been 2p and 5p coins in the change as £1.70 is divisible by ten. The only way then to make up the remaining £1.60 in 3 different coins is to have £1, 50p and 10p, Hence the change in coins is 1p, 1p, 1p, 2p, 5p, 10p, 50p and £1. So the two coins not given in change are £2 and 20p.

Question 12: D

If we express the speed of each train as W ms^{-1}. Then the relative speed of the two trains is 2W ms^{-1}.
Using Speed=distance/time: 2W = (140 + 140)/ 14.
Thus, 2W = 20, and W = 10. Thus, the speed of each train is 10 ms^{-1}.
To convert from metres to kilometres, divide by 1,000. To convert from seconds to hours, divide by 3,600.
Therefore, the conversion factor is to divide by 1,000/3,600 = 10/36 = 5/18
Thus, to convert from ms^{-1} to kmph, multiply by 18/5. Therefore, the final speed of the train is 18/5 x 10 = 36km/hr.

Question 13: C
Taking the day to be 24 hours long, this means the first tap fills 1/6 of the pool in an hour, the second 1/48, the third $\frac{1}{72}$ and the fourth $\frac{1}{96}$.

Taking 288 as the lowest common denominator, this gives: $\frac{48}{288} + \frac{6}{288} + \frac{4}{288} + \frac{3}{288}$ which $= \frac{61}{288}$ full in one hour. Hence the pool will be $\frac{244}{288}$ full in 4 hours.

The pool fills by approximately $\frac{15}{288}$ every 15 minutes.

Thus, in 4 Hours 15: $\frac{244 + 15}{288} = \frac{249}{288}$

Thus, in 4 Hours 30: $\frac{244 + 30}{288} = \frac{274}{288}$

Thus, in 4 Hours 45: $\frac{244 + 45}{288} = \frac{289}{288}$

Question 14: B
Every day up until day 28 the ant gains a net distance of 1cm, so at the end of day 27 the ant is at 27cm height and therefore only 1cm below the top. On day 28 the 3cm the ant climbs in the day is enough to take it to the top of the ditch and so it is able to climb out.

Question 15: A
To solve this question three different sums are needed to use the information given to deduce the costs of the various items. With the information that 30 oranges cost £12, £12/30 = 40p per orange with the 20% discount, hence oranges must cost 50p at full price. With the information that 5 sausages and 10 oranges cost £8.50, we know that the oranges at a 10% discount account for 10 x 45p = £4.50 so 5 undiscounted sausages cost £4 so each full price sausage is £4/5 = 80p. Finally we know that 10 sausages and 10 apples cost £9, at 10% discount the sausages cost 72p each thus accounting for 10 x 72p = £7.20 of the £9, hence the 10 apples at a 10% discount must cost £1.80, so each apple costs 18p at 10% discount. So an apple is 20p full price. Now to add up the final total: 2 oranges + 13 sausages + 2 apples = (2 x 50p) + (13 x 72p) + (12 x 18p) = £12.52.

Question 16: C
If we take the number of haircuts per year to be x, the information we have can be shown:

Membership	Annual Fee	Cost per cut	Total Yearly cost
None	None	£60	60x
VIP	£125	£50	£125 + 50x
Executive VIP	£200	£45	£200 + 45x

As we know that changing to either membership option would cost the same for the year, we can express the cost for the year, y as;
VIP: y = £125 + 50x
Executive VIP: y = £200 + 45x
Therefore: £125 + 50x = £200 + 45x
Simplified   5x = £75, therefore the number of haircuts a year, x is 15.
Substituting in x, we can therefore work out:

Membership	Annual	Cost per	Total Yearly

	Fee	cut	cost
None	None	£60	£900
VIP	£125	£50	£875
Executive VIP	£200	£45	£875

Hence the amount saved by buying membership is **£25.**

Question 17: B

All thieves are criminals. So the circle must be fully inside the square, we are told judges cannot be criminals so the star must be completely separate from the other two.

Question 18: C

We are told that March and May have the same last number, which must be either 3 or 13. Taking the information from the question that one of the factors is related to the letters of the month names, we can interpret that 13 represents the M which starts both March and May. Therefore we know the rule is that the last number is the position of the starting letter. Knowing that there is another factor about the letters of the month that controls the code we can work out that one of the number may code for the number of letters. Which in March would be 5, which is the second letter, so we have the rule of the 2nd number. Finally through observation we may note that the first number codes for the months' relative position in the year. Hence the code of April will be 4, (for its position), 5 (for the number of letters in the name) and 1 for the position of the starting letter 'A') and so 451 is the code.

Question 19: D

If b is the number of years older than 5, and a the number of A*s, the money given to the children can be expressed:

£5 + £3b + £10a

Hence for Josie £5 + (£3 x 11) + (£10 x 9) = £128

We know that Carson receives £44 less yearly, and his b value is 13, so his amount can be expressed:

£5 + (£3 x 13) + (£10a) = £84

Simplified: £44 + £10a = £84

I.e. £10a = £40,

So Carson's 'a' value, i.e. his number of A*s is 4, so the difference between Josie and Carson is **5.**

Question 20: B & C

Using the information to make a diagram:

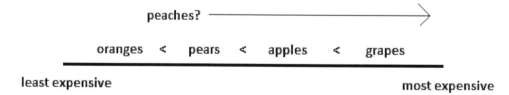

Hence **A** is incorrect. **D** and **E** may be true but we do not have enough information to say for sure. **B** is correct as we know peaches are more expensive than oranges but not about their price relative to pears. Equally we know **C** to be true as grapes are more expensive than apples so they must be more expensive than pears.

Question 21: B

It's easy to assume all the cuts should be in the vertical plane as a cake is usually sliced, however there is a way to achieve this with fewer cuts. Only three cutting motions are needed. **Start by cutting in the horizontal plane** through the centre of the cake to divide the top half from the bottom half. Then slice in the vertical plane into quarters to give 8 equally sized pieces with just three cuts.

Question 22: B & D

After the changes have been made, at 12 PM (GMT +1):
- Russell thinks it is 11 AM
- Tom thinks it is 12 PM

– Mark thinks it is 1 PM

Thus, in current GMT+1 time zone, Mark will arrive an hour early at 11 AM, Russell an hour late at 1 PM and Tom on time at 12 PM. There is therefore a two hour difference between the first and last arrival. For options E and F, be careful: the time zone listed is **NOT** GMT +1 that everyone else is working in. 1PM in GMT +3 = 11am GMT +1 (the summer time zone just entered) so that is Mark's actual arrival time; 12pm GMT +0 is the old time zone that Russell didn't change out of so that is Russell's correct arrival time.

Question 23: D

Using Bella's statements, as she must contradicted herself with her two statements, as one of them must be true, we know that it was definitely either Charlotte or Edward. Looking to the other statements, e.g. Darcy's we know that it was either Charlotte or Bella, as only one of the two statements saying it was both of them can have been a lie. Hence it must have been Charlotte.

Question 24: F

The only way to measure 0.1 litres or 100ml, is to fill the 300ml beaker, pour into the half litre/ 500 ml beaker, fill the 300ml again and pour (200ml) into the 500ml, which will make it full, leaving 100ml left in the 300ml beaker. The process requires 600ml of solution to fill the 300ml beaker twice.

Question 25: D

If you know how many houses there are on the street it is possible to work out the average, which then you can round up and down and to find the sequence of number, e.g. if you know there are 6 houses in the street 870/ 6 = 145. Which is not a house number because they are even so going up and down one even number consequentially one discovers that the numbers are 146, 144, 148, 150, 142 and 140. But it is not possible to determine Francis' house number without knowing its relative position i.e. highest, 3rd highest, lowest etc.

Question 26: D

Expressed through time:

Event	People Present
There were 20 people exercising in the cardio room	20
Four people were about to leave	20
A doctor was on the machine beside him (one of the original 20)	20
Emerging from his office one of the personal trainers called an ambulance.	21
Half of the people who were leaving, left (-2)	19
Eight people came into the room to hear the man being pronounced dead. (+8)	27
the two paramedics arrived, (+2)	29
the man was pronounced dead (-1)	28

Question 27: B & D

Blood loss can be described as 0.2 L/min.
For the man:
8 litres – 40% (3.2 L) = 4.8 L When he collapses, taking 16 minutes (3.2 / 0.2 = 16)
For the woman:
7 litres – 40% (2.8L) = 4.2: when she collapses, taking 14 minutes (2.8 / 0.2 = 14)
Hence the woman collapses 2 minutes before the man so **B** is correct, and **A** is incorrect. The total blood loss is 3.2L + 2.8L which = 6L so **C** is incorrect. The man's blood loss is 3.2L when he collapses so **E** is incorrect. The woman has a remaining blood volume of 4.2L when she collapses so **D** is correct. Blood loss is 0.2 L/min, which equates to 5 minutes per litre, which is 10 minutes per 2 litres not 12 L, so **F** is incorrect.

Question 28: B

Work out the times taken by each girl – (distance/pace) x 60 (converts to minutes) + lag time to start
Jenny: (13/8) x 60 = 97.5 minutes
Helen: (13/10) x 60 + 15 = 93 minutes
Rachel (13/11) x 60 + 25 = 95.9 minutes

Question 29: C

Work through each statement and the true figures.
A. Overlap of pain and flu-like symptoms must be at least 4% (56+48-100). 4% of 150: 0.04 x 150=6

B. 30% high blood pressure and 20% diabetes, so max percentage with both must be 20%. 20% of 150: 0.2*150 = 30

C. Total number of patients – patients with flu-like symptoms – patients with high blood pressure. Assume different populations to get min number without either. 150 – (0.56 x 150) – (0.3 x 150) = 21

D. This is an obvious trap that you might fall into if you added up the percentages and noted that the total was >100%. However, this isn't a problem as patients can discussed two problems.

Question 30: C

This is easiest to work out if you give all products an original price, I have used £100. You can then work out the higher price, and the subsequent sale price, and thus the discount from the original £100 price. As the price increases and decreases are in percentages, they will be the same for all items regardless of the price so it does not matter what the initial figure you start with is.

Marked up price: 100 x 1.15 = £115

Sale price: 115 x 0.75 = £86.25

Percentage reduction from initial price is 100 – 86.25 = 13.75%

Question 31: D

The recipe states 2 eggs makes 12 pancakes, therefore each egg makes 6 pancakes, so the number Steve must make should be a multiple of 6 to ensure he uses a whole egg.

Steve requires a minimum of 15 x 3 = 45 pancakes. To ensure use of whole eggs, this should be increased to 48 pancakes.

The original recipe is for 12 pancakes, therefore to make 48 pancakes, require 4x recipe (48/12).

Therefore quantities: 8 eggs, 400g plain flour and 1200 ml milk.

Question 32: B

Work through the question backwards.

In 6 litres of diluted bleach, there are 4.8 litres of water and 1.2 litres of partially diluted bleach.

In the 1.2 litres of partially diluted bleach, there is 9 parts water to one part original warehouse bleach. Remember that a ratio of 1:9 means 1/10 bleach and 9/10 water. Therefore working through, there is 120ml of warehouse bleach needed.

Question 33: C

We know that Charles is born in 2002, therefore in 2010 he must be 8. There are 3 years between Charles and Adam, and Charles is the middle grandchild. As Bertie is older than Adam, Adam must be younger than Charles so Adam must be 5 in 2010. In 2010, if Adam is 5, Bertie must be 10 (states he is double the age of Adam). The question asks for ages in 2015: Adam = 10, Bertie = 15, Charles = 13

Question 34: B

Make the statements into algebraic equations and then solve them as you would simultaneous equations. Let a denote the flat fixed rate for hire, and b the price per half hour.

Cost = a + b(time in mins/30)

Peter: a + 6b (6 half hours) = 14.50 (equation 1)

Kevin: 2a + 18b = 41, or this can be simplified to give cost per kayak, a + 9b = 20.5 (equation 2)

If you subtract equation 1 from equation 2:

3b = 6, therefore b = 2

Substitute b into either equation to calculate a, using equation 1, a + 12 = 14.50, therefore a = 2.50

Finally use these values to work out the cost for 2 hours:

2.50 (flat fee) + 4 x 2 (4half hours x cost/half hour) = £10.50

Question 35: E

It is most helpful to write out all the numbers from 0 – 9 in digital format to most easily see which light elements are used for each number. You can then cross out any numbers which don't use all the lights from the digit 7.

Go through the digits methodically and you can cross out: 1, 2, 4, 5, and 6. These numbers don't contain all three bars from the digit 7.

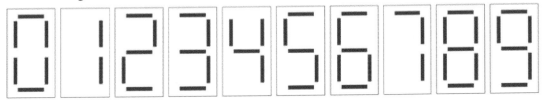

Question 36: B

In this question it is worth remembering it will take more people a shorter amount of time.

Work out how many man hours it takes to build the house. Days x hours x builders

12 x 7 x 4 = 336 hours

Work out how many hours it will take the 7man workforce: 336/7 = 48 hours

Convert to 8 hour days: 48/8 = 6 days

Question 37: D

By far the easiest way to do these type of questions is to draw a Venn diagram (use question marks if you are unsure about the exact position):

Now, it is a case of going through each statement:

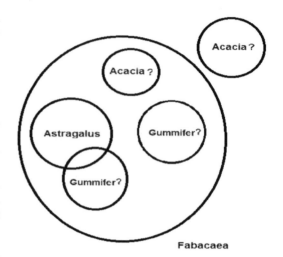

A. Incorrect - Acacia may be fabacaea. Acacia are not astragalus, but does not logically follow that they therefore can't be fabacaea.
B. Incorrect – astragalus and gummifer are not necessarily separate within fabacaea.
C. Incorrect – the statement is not reversible so the fact that all astragalus and gummifer are fabacaea does not mean all facacaea are gummifer and/or astragalus. E.g. Fabacaea could be acacia.
D. Correct
E. Incorrect – Whilst some acacia could be gummifer, there is no certainty that they are.

Question 38: D

Area of a trapezium = (a+b)/2 x h

Area of cushion = (50+30)/2 x 50 = 2000cm^2

Since each width of fabric is 1m wide, both sides of one cushion can fit into one width. The required length is therefore 75cm x 4 = 3m with a cost of 3 x £10 = £30.

Cost of seamstress = £25 x 4 = £100

Total cost is £130

Question 39: C

There are 30 days in September, so Lisa will buy 30 coffees.

In Milk, every 10th coffee is free, so Lisa will pay for 27 coffees at 2.40 = £64.80

In Beans, Lisa gets 20 points each day and needs 220 points to get a free coffee, which is 11 days, with 5 points left over. Therefore, in 30 days she will get 2 free coffees. The cost for 28 coffees at 2.15 is £60.20

Beans is cheaper, and the difference is £64.80 - £60.20 = £4.60.

Question 40: C

Work backwards and take note of how often each bus comes.

Must get off 220 bus at 10.57 latest. Can get 10.40 bus therefore (arrive at 10.54).

Latest can get on 283 bus is 10.15 as to make the 220 bus connection. 283 comes every 10mins (question doesn't state at what points past the hour), so Paula should be at the bus stop at 10.06 to ensure a bus comes by 10.15 at the latest. If the bus comes every 10mins, even if a bus comes at 10.05 which Paula will miss, the next bus will come at 10.15 and therefore she will still be on time.

Therefore Paula must leave at 10.01

Question 41: B
You are working out the time taken to reach the same distance (D). Make sure to take into account changing speeds of train A, and that train B leaves 20 minutes earlier.

$$Speed = \frac{distance}{time}$$

Make sure you keep the answers consistent in the time units you are using, the worked answer is all in minutes (hence the need to multiply by 60).

Train A: time for first $20km = \dfrac{20}{100} x \, 60 = 12 \, minutes$

So the distance where it equals B is $12 + (\dfrac{D - 20}{150}) \, x \, 60$

You need to use D-20 to account for the fact you have already calculated the time at the slower speed for the first 20km

Train B: $\dfrac{(\frac{D}{90}) \, x \, 60}{} - 20$

Make the equations equal each other as they describe the same time and distance, and solve.

Simplifies to $32 + \dfrac{2D}{5} - 8 = \dfrac{2D}{3}$ so $D = 90km$

Train B will take 60 minutes to travel 90 km and train A will take 40 minutes (but as it leaves 20 minutes later, this will be point at which it passes).

Question 42: C
Work out the annual cost of local gym: 12 x 15 = £180
Upfront cost + class costs of university gym must therefore be >£180.
Subtract upfront cost to find number of classes: 180 – 35 = £145
Divide by cost per class (£3) to find number of classes: 145/3 = 48 1/3
48 1/3 classes would make the two gyms the same price, so for the local gym to be cheaper, you would need to attend 49 classes.

Question 43: C
A is definitely true, since the question states that all herbal drugs are not medicines. **B** is also definitely true as all antibiotics are medicines which are all drugs. **C** is definitely false, because all antibiotics are medicine, yet no herbal drugs are medicines. **D** is true as all antibiotics are medicines.

Question 44: C
Answer **A** cannot be reliably concluded, because from the information given a non-"Fast" train could stop at Newark, but not at Northallerton or Durham. We have no information on whether *all* trains stopping at Newark also stop at Northallerton.

Answer **B** is not correct because 8 is the *average* number of trains that stop at Northallerton. It is possible that on some days more than 16 trains run, and more than 8 will thus stop at Northallerton. Answer **D** is incorrect because it is mentioned that *all* trains stopping at Northallerton also stop at Durham, giving a total 6 stops as a minimum for a train stopping at Northallerton (the others being the 4 stops which *all* trains stop at).

Answer **E** is incorrect for a similar reason to **A**. We have no information on whether all trains stopping at Newark also stop at Northallerton, so cannot determine that they must also stop at Durham.

Answer **C** is correct because "Fast" trains make less than 5 stops. Since all trains already stop at 4 stops (Peterborough, York, Darlington and Newcastle), they cannot then stop at Durham, as this would give 5 stops.

Question 45: D

From the information we are given, we can compose the following image of how these towns are located (not to scale, but shows the direction of each town with respect to the others):

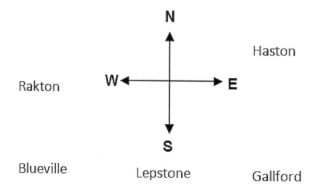

From this "map", we can see that all statements apart from **D** are true. Statement **D** is definitely *not true*, since Blueville is south west of Haston it cannot be East of Haston.

Question 46: C

We are told that in order to form a government, a party (or coalition) must have *over* 50% of seats. Thus, they must have at least 50% of the total seats plus 1, which is 301 seats.

We are told that we are looking for the *minimum* number of seats the greens can have in order to form a coalition with red and orange. Thus, we are seeking for Red and Orange to have the *maximum* number of seats possible, under the criteria given.

Thus we can calculate as follows:
- No party has over 45% of seats, so the maximum that the Red party can have is 45%, which is 270 seats.
- No party except for red and blue has won more than 4% of seats. We are told that the green party won the 4th highest number of seats, so it is possible that the Orange party won the 3rd highest.
- Thus, the maximum number of seats the orange party can have won is 4% of the total, which is 24 seats.
- Thus, the maximum possible combined total of the Red and Orange party's seats won is 294.

Thus, in order to achieve a total of 301 seats in a Red-Orange-Green coalition, the Green party have to have won at least 7 seats.

Question 47: E

Expressing the amount each child receives:

Youngest	M
2nd youngest	$M + D$
3rd youngest/ 3rd oldest	$M + 2D$
4th youngest/ 2nd oldest	$M + 3D$
Oldest	$M + 4D$

Question 48: D

The total amount of money received;
£100, $= M + M + D + M + 2D + M + 3D + M + 4D$
Simplified, thus is:
£100 $= 5M + 10D$

Question 49: C

The two youngest are expressed as M and $M + D$. Simplified as $2M + D$.
The three oldest are expressed as $M + 2D$, $M + 3D$ and $M + 4D$, Simplified as $3M + 9D$
Hence 7 times the two youngest together is expressed $7(2M + D)$, so altogether the Answer is $7(2M + D) = 3M + 9D$.

Question 50: A

To work this out, simplify the two equations:

$7(2M + D) = 3M + 9D$

$14M + 7D = 3M + 9D$

$11M = 2D$

$M = \dfrac{2D}{11}$

Question 51: A

Substitute M into the equation $£100 = 5M + 10D$

$5\left(\dfrac{2D}{11}\right) + 10D = £100$

$\dfrac{10D}{11} + 10D = \dfrac{10D}{11} + \dfrac{110D}{11} = \dfrac{120D}{11}$

Question 52: C & E

The easiest way to work this out is using a table. With the information we know:

1ˢᵗ		Madeira
2ⁿᵈ		
3ʳᵈ	Jaya	
4ᵗʰ		

Ellen made carrot cake and it was not last. It now cannot be 1ˢᵗ or 3rd as these places are taken so it must be second:

1ˢᵗ		Madeira
2ⁿᵈ	Ellen	Carrot cake
3ʳᵈ	Jaya	
4ᵗʰ		

Aleena's was better than the tiramisu, so she can't have come last, therefore Aleena must have placed first

1ˢᵗ	Aleena	Madeira
2ⁿᵈ	Ellen	Carrot cake
3ʳᵈ	Jaya	
4ᵗʰ		

And the girl who made the Victoria sponge was better than Veronica:

1ˢᵗ	Aleena	Madeira
2ⁿᵈ	Ellen	Carrot cake
3ʳᵈ	Jaya	Victoria Sponge
4ᵗʰ	Veronica	Tiramisu

Question 53: D

The information given can be expressed to show the results that the teams must have had to make their points total.

Team	Points	Game Results			
Celtic Changers	2	L	L	D	D
Eire Lions	?	?	?	?	?
Nordic Nesters	8	W	W	D	D
Sorten Swipers	5	W	D	D	L
Whistling	1	D	L	L	L

Winners

The results so far total 3 wins, 6 losses and 7 draws. Since, the number of draws must be even, there must have been another draw. So we know one of the Eire Lions results is a draw.

The difference between wins (3) and losses (6) is 3. Thus, there must be another 3 wins to account for this difference. So the Eire Lions results must be 3 wins and 1 draw. Thus, they scored 3 x 3 + 1 = 10.

Question 54: D

Remember to consider the gender of each person. Then draw a quick diagram to show the given information you can see that only D is correct.

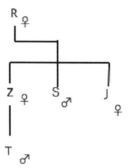

Question 55: B

After the first round; he knocks off 8 bottles to leave 8 left on the shelf. He then puts back 4 bottles. There are therefore 12 left on the shelf. After the second round, he has hit 3 bottles and damages 6 bottles in total, and an additional 2 at the end. He then puts up 2 new bottles to leave 12 – 8 + 2 = 6 bottles left on the shelf. After the final round, John knocks off 3 bottles from the shelf to leave 3 bottles standing.

Question 56: D

Based on the information we have we can plot the travel times below. Change over times are in a smaller font.

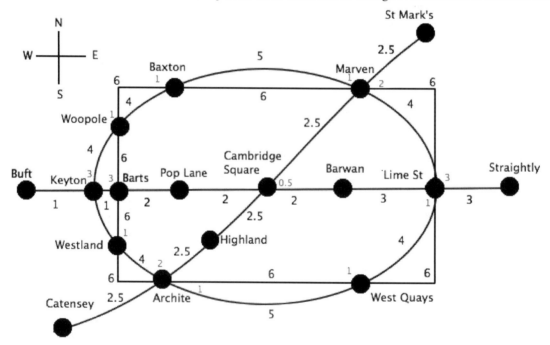

Hence on the St Mark's line, St Mark's to Archite takes 4 x 2.5 minutes = 10 minutes.

Question 57: A

Going from stop to stop on the Straightly line end Buft to Straightly would take 14 minutes, but we are told earlier on there is an express train that goes end to end and only takes 6.

Question 58: B

The quickest route from Baxton to Pop Lane is via Marven and Cambridge Square, which takes 5 + 2 + 2.5 + 0.5 + 2 = 12 minutes. Baxton to Pop Lane via Barts would take 4 + 1 + 6 + 3 + 2 = 16 minutes, which is longer so **E** is incorrect. Other options include times failing to take account of, or incorrectly adding changeover times, and so are incorrect.

Question 59: C

From Cambridge Square:

➢ Catensey is (2.5 x 3 =) 7.5 minutes away.
➢ Woopole, is (4 + 3 + 1 +2 + 2 =) 12 minutes.
➢ Buft is (1 + 1 + 2 + 2 =) 6 minutes.
➢ Westland is (4 + 2 + 2.5 + 2.5 =) 11 minutes.

Question 60: B

With the new delay information we can plot the travel times as before, adjusted for the delays. Plus a 5 minute delay on the platforms when waiting on any platform for a train.

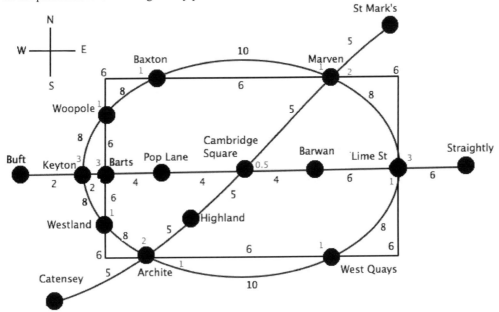

The quickest way from Westland to Marven now uses the non-delayed reliable rectangle line. Four stops on the rectangle line take 6 mins each so 24 minutes in total on the train. Add to this the additional 5 minutes platform waiting time to give a total journey time of 29 minutes.

Question 61: C

- Baxton to Archite via Barts using only the Rectangle line takes (5 + 6 +6+ 6 +6=) 29 minutes.
- Baxton to Woopole on the Rectangle line, then Oval to Archite via Keyton takes (5 + 6 + 1 + 5 + 8 + 8 + 8 =) 41 minutes
- Baxton to Archite on the Oval line only takes (5 + (8 x 4) =) 37 minutes
- Baxton to Woopole on the Oval line, then Rectangle to Archite via Barts takes (5 + 8 + 1 + 5 + 6 + 6 + 6 =) 37 minutes
- As the bus takes 27-31 minutes, it is not possible to tell from between the options which will be slower/quicker so option **C** is the right answer.

Question 62: D

Remember the 5-minute platform wait. We are not told that the St Mark's express train from end to end is no longer running so we must assume that it is, which takes 5 minutes (plus the wait at St Mark's to go to Catensey).

Then, there is a 5 minute wait at Catensey to Archite, and a 2 + 5 minute changeover at Archite onto the Rectangle line which then takes 6 minutes to West Quays. 5 + 5 + 5 + 5 + 2 + 5 + 6

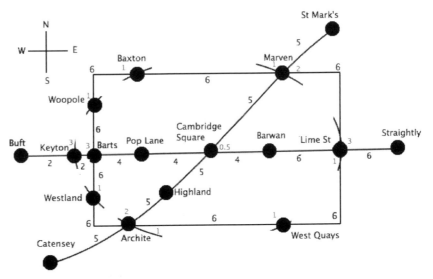

= 33 minutes. Via Lime St the journey takes 5 + 5 + 5+ 2 + 5 + 6+ 6 = 29 minutes.

Question 63: D

From the information:

- "Simon's horse wore number 1."
- "..the horse that wore 3, which was wearing red.."
- "the horse wearing blue wore number 4."

We can plot the information below:

Place	Owner	Number	Colours
	Simon	1	
		2	
		3	Red
		4	Blue

In addition: "The horse wearing green; Celia's, came second"

Which means Celia's horse must have worn number two because it cannot have worn number 1 because that is Simon's horse. Also it cannot have worn number three or four because they wore red and blue respectively. So we can plot this further deduction:

Place	Owner	Number	Colours
	Simon	1	
2nd	Celia	2	Green
		3	Red
		4	Blue

We also know that

- "Arthur's horse beat Simon's horse"
- "Celia's horse beat the horse that wore number 1." i.e. Simon's

We know Celia's horse came second, and that both Celia's and Arthur's horses beat Simon's. This means that Simon's horse must have come last. So;

Place	Owner	Number	Colours
4th	Simon	1	
2nd	Celia	2	Green
		3	Red
		4	Blue

And knowing that:

- "Only one horse wore the same number as the position it finished in."

The horses wearing numbers 3 and 4 must have placed 1st and 3rd respectively. Hence:

Place	Owner	Number	Colours
4th	Simon	1	
2nd	Celia	2	Green
1st		3	Red
3rd		4	Blue

"Lila's horse wasn't painted yellow nor blue"

So Lila's must have been red, and Simon's yellow. Leaving the only option for Arthur's to be blue. So we now know:

Place	Owner	Number	Colours
4th	Simon	1	Yellow
2nd	Celia	2	Green

| 1st | Lila | 3 | Red |
| 3rd | Arthur | 4 | Blue |

Question 64: C

Year 1 – 40 x 1.2 = 48

Year 2 – 48 x 1.2 = 57.6

Year 3 – 57.6 x 1.1 = 63.36

Year 4 – 63.36 x 1.1 = 69.696.

Question 65: C

To minimise the total cost to the company, they want the wage bills for each site to be less than £200,000. Working this out involves some trial and error; you can speed this up by splitting employees who earn similar amounts between the sites e.g. Nicola and John as they are the top two earners.

Nicola + Daniel + Luke = £ 198,500 and John + Emma + Victoria = £ 199,150

Question 66: C

Remember that pick up and drop off stops may be the same stop, therefore the minimum number of stops the bus had to make was 7. This would take 7 x 1.5 = 10.5 minutes.

Therefore the total journey time = 24 + 10.5 = 34.5 minutes.

Question 67: A

The best method here is to work backwards. We know the potatoes have to be served immediately, so they should be finished roasting at 4pm, so they should start roasting 50 minutes prior to that, at 3:10. We also know they have to be roasted immediately after boiling, so they should be prepared by 3:05, in order to boil in time. She should therefore start preparing them no later than 2:47, though she could prepare them earlier.

The chicken needs to be cooked by 3:55 to give it time to stand, so it should begin roasting at 2:40, and Sally should begin to prepare it no later than 2:25.

You can construct a rough timeline:

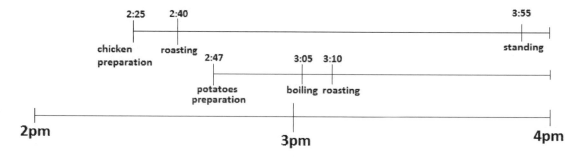

We can see from this timeline that from 2:40 onwards, there will be no long enough period of time in which there is a free space in the cooker for the vegetables to be boiled. They therefore must be finished cooking at 3:05. The latest time prior to this that Sally has time to prepare them (5 minutes) is at 2:40, between preparing the chicken and the potatoes. She should therefore begin preparing the vegetables at 2:42, then begin boiling at 2:47, so they can be finished cooking by 2:55, in time for the potatoes to boil at 3:05.

Chicken: 2:25

Potatoes: 2:47

Vegetables: 2:42

Question 68: C
The quickest way to do this is via trial and error. However, for the sake of completion: let each child's age be denoted by the letter of their name, and form an equation for their total age:

$P + J + A + R = 80$

The age of each child can be written in terms of Paul's age.

P = 2J, therefore $J = \dfrac{P}{2}$

$A = \dfrac{P + J}{2}$

Now substitute in $J = \dfrac{P}{2}$ to get in terms of P only: $A = \dfrac{P + \dfrac{P}{2}}{2} = \dfrac{P}{2} + \dfrac{P}{4} = \dfrac{3P}{4}$

$R = P + 2$

Thus: $P + \dfrac{P}{2} + \dfrac{3P}{4} + P(+ 2) = 80$

Simplify to give: $\dfrac{13P}{4} = 78$

$13P = 312$. Thus, $P = 24$

Substitute P = 24 into the equations for the other children to get: J = 12, A = 18, R = 26

Question 69: A
The total number of buttons is 71 + 86 + 83 = 240. The total number of suitable buttons is 22 + 8 = 30. Thus, she will have to remove a maximum of 210 buttons in order to guarantee picking a suitable button on the next attempt.

Question 70: E
This question requires you to calculate the adjusted score for Ben for each segment. If Ben has a 50% chance of hitting the segment he is aiming for, we can assume he hits each adjacent segment 25% of the time. Thus:

$Adjusted\ Score = \dfrac{Segment\ aimed\ at}{2} + \dfrac{First\ Adjacent\ Segment}{4} + \dfrac{Second\ Adjacent\ Segment}{4}$

$Adjusted\ Score = \dfrac{Segment\ aimed\ at}{2} + \dfrac{Sum\ of\ Adjacent\ Segments}{4}$

E.g. if he aims at segment 1: He will score $\dfrac{1}{2} + \dfrac{18 + 20}{4} = 10$

Now it is a simple case of trying the given options to see which segment gives the highest score. In this case, it is segment 19: $\dfrac{19}{2} + \dfrac{7 + 3}{4} = 12$

Question 71: C
The total cost is £8.75, and Victoria uses a £5.00 note, leaving a total cost of £3.65 to be paid using change.
Up to 20p can be paid using 1p and 2p pieces, so she could use 20 1p coins to make up this amount.
Up to 50p can be paid using 5p and 10p pieces, so she could use 10 5p pieces to make up this amount. This gives a total of 30 coins, and a total payment of £0.70.
Up to £1.00 can be paid using 20p pieces and 50p pieces. Thus, she could use up to 5 20p pieces, giving a total of 35 coins used, and a total payment of £1.70.

The smallest denomination of coin that can now be used is a £1.00 coin. Hence Victoria must use 2 £1.00 coins, giving a total of 37 coins, and a total payment of £3.70. However, we know that the total cost to pay in change was £3.65, and that Victoria paid the exact amount, receiving no change. Thus, we must take away coins to the value of 5p, removing the smallest number of coins possible. This is achieved by taking away 1 5p piece, giving a grand total of 36 coins.

Question 72: B

The time could be 21:25, if first 2 digits were reversed by the glass of water (21 would be reversed to give 15). **A** cannot be the answer, because this would involve altering the last 2 digits, and we can see that 25 on a digital clock, when reversed simply gives 25 (the 2 on the left becomes a 5 on the right, and the 5 on the right becomes a 2 on the left). **C** cannot be the answer, as this involves reversing the middle 2 digits. As with the right two digits, the middle 2 digits of 2:5 would simply reverse to give itself, 2:5. **D** could be the time if the 2nd and 4th digits were reversed, as they would both become 2's. However, the question says that 2 *adjacent* digits are reversed, meaning that the 2nd and 4th digits cannot be reversed as required here. **E** is not possible as it would require all four numbers to be reversed.

Thus, the answer is **B**.

Question 73: B

We can see from the question that Lorkdon is a democracy and therefore cannot have been invaded by a democracy because of the treaty (we are assuming this treaty is upheld, as said in the question). Thus, Nordic (which has invaded Lorkdon) *must* be a dictatorship. Now, we can see that Worsid has been invaded by a dictatorship, *and* has invaded a dictatorship. The question states that no dictatorship has undergone both of these events. Thus, we know that Worsid cannot be a dictatorship. We also know from the question that each of these countries is *either* a dictatorship or a democracy. Thus, Worsid must be a democracy.

Question 74: C

The total price of all of these items would usually be £17. However, with the DVD offer, the customer saves £1, giving a total cost of £16. Thus, the customer will need to receive £34 in change.

Question 75: B

To answer this, we simply calculate how much total room in the pan will be taken up by the food for each guest:
- 2 rashers of bacon, giving a total of 14% of the available space.
- 4 sausages, taking up a total of 12% of the available space.
- 1 egg takes up 12% of the available space.

Adding these figures together, we see that each guest's food takes up a total of 38% of the available space.

Thus, Ryan can only cook for 2 guests at once, since 38% multiplied by 3 is 114%, and we cannot use up more than 100% of the available space in the pan.

Question 76: C

To calculate this, let the total number of employees be termed "Y".

We can see that £60 is the total cost for providing cakes for 40% of "Y".

We know that £2 is required for each cake. Thus, we can work out that 30 must be 40% of Y.

$0.4Y = 60/2$
$0.4Y = 30$
$Y = 75$

Thus, we can calculate that the total number of employees must be 75.

Question 77: E

The normal waiting time for treatment is 3 weeks. However, the higher demand in Bob's local district mean this waiting time is extended by 50%, giving a total of 4.5 weeks.

Then, we must consider the delay induced because Bob is a lower risk case, which extends the waiting time by another 20%. 20% of 4.5 is 0.9, so there is a delay of another 0.9 weeks for treatment.

Thus, Bob can expect to wait 5.4 weeks for specialist treatment on his tumour.

Question 78: D

In the class of 30, 40% drink alcohol at least once a month, which is 12. Of these, 75% drink alcohol once a week, which is 9. Of these, 1 in 3 smoke marijuana, which is 3.

In the class of 30, 60% drink alcohol less than once a month, which is 18. Of these, 1 in 3 smoke marijuana, which is 6.

Therefore the total number of students who smoke marijuana is 3+6, which is 9.

Question 79: C

The sequence can either be thought of as doubling the previous number then adding 2, or adding 1 then doubling. Double 46 is 92, plus 2 is 94.

Question 80: B

If the mode of 5 numbers of 3, it must feature at least two threes. If the median is 8, we know that the 3rd largest number is an 8. Hence we know that the 3 smallest numbers are 3, 3, and 8. Because the mean is 7, we know that the 5 numbers must add up to 35. The three smallest numbers add up to 14. Hence the two largest must add up to 21.

Question 81: E

The biggest difference in the weight of potatoes will be if the bag with only 5 potatoes in weighs the maximum, 1100g, and the bag with 10 potatoes weighs the minimum, 900g. If there are 5 equally heavy potatoes in a bag weighing 1100g, each weighs 220g. If there are 10 equally heavy potatoes in a 900g bag, each weighs 90g. The difference between these is 130g.

Question 82: D

There are 60 teams, and 4 teams in each group, so there are 15 groups. In each group, if each team plays each other once, there will be 6 matches in each group, making a total of 90 matches in the group stage. There are then 16 teams in the knockout stages, so 8 matches in the first round knockout, then 4, then 2, then 1 final match when only two teams are left. Hence there are 105 matches altogether ($90 + 8 + 4 + 2 + 1 = 105$).

Question 83: A

We know the husband's PIN number must be divisible by 8 because it has been multiplied by 2 3 times and had a multiple of 8 added to it. The largest 4 digit number which is divisible by 8 is 9992. Minus 200 is 9792. Divide by 2 is 4896. Hence the largest the husband's last 4 card digits can be is 4896. Minus 200 is 4696. Divide by 2 is 2348. Hence the largest my last 4 card digits can be is 2348. Minus 200 is 2148. Divide by 2 is 1074. Hence the largest my PIN number can be is 1074.

Question 84: C

If the first invitation is sent as early as possible, it will be sent on the 50th birthday. It will be accepted after 2 reminders and hence conducted at 50 years 11 months. The time between each screening will be 3 years 11 months. Hence, the second screening will be at 54 years 10 months. The third screening will be at 58 years 9 months. Hence, the fourth screening will be at 62 years 8 months.

Question 85: A

Ellie has worked for the company for more than five but less than six whole years. At the end of each whole year she receives a pay rise in thousands equal to the number of years of her tenure. Therefore at the end of the first year the raise is £1,000, then at the end of the second year it is £2,000 and so on to year 5. Thus the total amount of her pay comprised by the pay rises is £15,000, so the basic pay before accounting for these rises was £40,000 - £15,000 = £25,000.

Question 86: B

The trains come into the station together every 40 minutes, as the lowest common multiple of 2, 5 and 8 is 40. Hence, if the last time trains came together was 15 minutes ago, the next time will be in 25 minutes.

Question 87: C

If you smoke, your risk of getting Disease X is 1 in 24. If you drink alcohol, your risk of getting Disease X is 1 in 6. Each tablet of the drug halves your risk. Therefore a drinker taking 1 tablet means their risk is 1 in 12, and taking 2 tablets means their risk is 1 in 24, the same as someone who smokes.

Question 88: A

There are 10 red and 8 green balls. Clearly the most likely combination involves these colours only. Since there are more red balls than green, the probability of red-red is greater than green-green. However, there are **two** possible ways to draw a combination, either the red first followed by green or green first followed by red. The

probability of red-red $= \left(\dfrac{10}{20}x\dfrac{9}{19}\right) = \dfrac{9}{38}$.

The probability of red and green = $\left(\frac{8}{20} \times \frac{10}{19}\right) + \left(\frac{10}{20} \times \frac{8}{19}\right) = \frac{8}{38} + \frac{8}{38} = \frac{16}{38}$. Therefore the combination of red and green is more likely.

Question 89: B

The least likely combination of balls to draw is blue and yellow. You are much more likely to draw a green ball than either a blue or yellow one because there are many more in the bag. Since the draw is taken without replacement, yellow and yellow is impossible because there is only one yellow ball.

Question 90: F

Since there is only 1 blue and 1 yellow ball, it is possible to take 18 balls which are red or green. You would need to take 19 of the 20 balls to be certain of getting either the blue ball or the yellow ball.

Question 91: C

The smallest number of parties required would theoretically be 3 – Namely Labour, the Liberal Democrats and UKIP, giving a total of 355 seats. However, the Liberal Democrats will not form a coalition with UKIP, so this will not be possible. Thus, there are 2 options:

➢ Labour can form a coalition with the Greens and UKIP, which is not contradictory to anything mentioned in the question. This would give a total of 325 seats, and would thus need the next 2 largest parties (The Scottish National Party and Plaid Cymru) in order to get more than 350 seats, meaning 5 parties would need to be involved.
➢ Alternatively, Labour can form a coalition with the Liberal Democrats and the Green Party. This would give a total of 340 seats. Only one more party (e.g. the Scottish National Party) would be required to exceed 350 seats, giving a grand total of 4 parties.

Thus, the smallest number of parties needed to form a coalition would be 4.

Question 92: E

360 appointments are attended and only 90% of those booked are attended, meaning there were originally 400 appointments booked in and 40 have been missed. 1 in 2 of the booked appointments were for male patients, so 200 appointments were for male patients. Male patients are three times as likely to miss booked appointments, so of the 40 that were missed, 30 were missed by men. Given that of 200 booked appointments, 30 were missed, this means 170 were attended.

Question 93: B

If every one of 60 students studies 3 subjects, this is 180 subject choices altogether. 60 of these are Maths, because everyone takes Maths. 60% of 60 is 36, so 36 are Biology. 50% of 60 is 30, so 30 are Economics and 30 are Chemistry. 60+36+30+30=156, so there are 24 subject choices left which must be Physics.

Question 94: B

If 100,000 people are diagnosed with chlamydia and 0.6 partners are informed each, this is 60,000 people, of which 80% (so 48,000) have tests. 12,000 of the partners who are informed, as well as 240,000 who are not (300,000 – 60,000) do not have tests. This makes 252,000 who are not tested. We can assume that half of these people would have tested positive for chlamydia, which is 126,000. So the answer is 126,000.

Question 95: C

Tiles can be added at either end of the 3 lines of 2 tiles horizontally or at either end of the 2 lines of 2 tiles vertically. This is a total of 10, but in two cases these positions are the same (at the bottom of the left hand vertical line and the top of the right hand vertical line). So the answer is $10 - 2 = 8$.

Question 96: C

Harry needs a total of 4000ml + 1200ml = 5200ml of squash. He has 1040ml of concentrated squash, which is a fifth of the total dilute squash he needs. So he will need 4 parts water to every 1 part concentrated squash, therefore the resulting liquid is 1/5 squash and 4/5 water.

Question 97: C

There are 24 different possible arrangements (4 x 3 x 2 x 1), which means that there are 23 other possible arrangements than Alex, Beth, Cathy, Daniel.

Question 98: F

A is incorrect because the distance travelled is only 10 miles. **B** is incorrect because the distance travelled is 19 miles. **C** is incorrect because no town is visited twice. **D** is incorrect because Hondale and Baleford are both visited twice. **E** is incorrect because no town is visited twice. Therefore **F** is the correct answer.

Question 99: C

Georgia is shorter than her Mum and Dad, and each of her siblings is at least as tall as Mum (and we know Mum is shorter than Dad because Ellie is between the two), so we know Georgia is the shortest. We know that Ellie, Tom and Dad are all taller than Mum, so Mum is second shortest. Ellie is shorter than Dad and Tom is taller than Dad, so we can work out that Ellie must be third shortest.

Question 100: A

Danielle must be sat next to Caitlin. Bella must be sat next to the teaching assistant. Hence these two pairs must sit in different rows. One pair must be sat at the front with Ashley, and the other must be sat at the back with Emily. Since the teaching assistant has to sit on the left, this must mean that Bella is sat in the middle seat and either Ashley or Emily (depending on which row they are in) is sat in the right hand seat. However, Bella cannot sit next to Emily, so this means Bella and the teaching assistant must be in the front row. So Ashley must be sat in the front right seat.

Question 101: C

The dishwasher is run 2+p times a week, where p is the number of people in the house. Let the number of people in the house when the son is not home be s, and when the son is home it is s+1. In 30 weeks when the son is home, she would buy 6 packs of dishwasher tablets. In 30 weeks when the son is not home, she would buy 5 packs of dishwasher tablets. So 1.2 times as many packs of dishwasher tablets are bought when he is home. So 2+s+1 is 1.2 time 2+s.

i.e. $2.4 + 1.2s = 2 + s + 1$

Therefore 0.2s = 0.6

s = 3

When her son is home, there are s + 1 = 4 people in the house.

Question 102: A

No remaining days in the year obey the rule. The next date that does is 01/01/2015 (integers are 0, 1, 2, 5). This is 6 days later than the specified date.

Question 103: B

If each town is due North, South, East or West of at least 2 other towns and we know that one is east and one is north of a third, then they must be arranged in a square. So Yellowtown is 4 miles east of Bluetown to make a square, which means it must be 5 miles north of Redtown. So Redtown is 5 miles south of Yellowtown.

Question 104: B

Jenna pours 4/5 of 250 ml into each glass, which is 200 ml. Since she has 1500 ml of wine, she pours 100 ml into the last glass, which is 2/5 of the 250 ml full capacity.

Question 105: E

The maximum number of girls in Miss Ellis's class with brown eyes and brown hair is 10, because the two thirds of the girls with brown eyes could also all have brown hair. The minimum number is 0 because it could be that all the boys, and the third of the girls without brown eyes, all had brown hair, which would be 2/3 of the class.

Question 106: E

A negative "score" results from any combination of throws which includes a 1 but from no other combination. Given that a negative score has a 0.75 probability, a positive or zero score has a 0.25 probability. Therefore throwing two numbers that are not 1 twice in a row has a probability of 0.25. Hence, the probability of throwing a non-1 number on each throw is $\sqrt{0.25} = 0.5$. So the probability of throwing a 1 on an individual throw is $1 - 0.5 = 0.5$.

Question 107: C
We can work out from the information given the adult flat rate and the charge per stop. Let the charge per stop be s and the flat rate be f. Therefore: 15s + f = 1.70
8s + f = 1.14
We can hence work out that: 7s = 0.56, so s = 0.08. Hence, f = 0.50
Megan is an adult so she pays this rate. For 30 stops, the rate will be 0.08 x 30 + 0.50 = 2.90.

Question 108: B
We found in the previous question that the flat rate for adults is £0.50 and the rate per stop is £0.08. We know that the child rate is half the flat rate and a quarter of the "per stop" rate, so the child flat rate is £0.25 and the rate per stop is 2p. So for 25 stops, Alice pays:
0.02 x 25 + 0.25 = 0.75

Question 109: C
We should first work out how many stops James can travel. For £2, he can afford to travel as many stops as £1.50 will take him once the flat rate is taken into account. The per stop rate is 8p per stop, so he can travel 18 stops, so he will need to go to the 18th stop from town. So he will need to walk past 7 stops to get to the stop he can afford to travel from.

Question 110: D
The picture will need a 12 inch by 16 inch mount, which will cost £8. It will need a 13 inch by 17 inch frame, which will cost £26. So the cost of mounting and framing the picture will be £8 + £26 = £34.

Question 111: C
Mounting and framing an 8 by 8 inch painting will cost £5 for the mount and £22 for the frame, which is £27. Mounting and framing a 10 by 10 inch painting will cost £6 for the mount and £26 for the frame, which is £32. The difference is £32 - £27 = £5.

Question 112: B
We found in the last question that mounting and framing a 10 by 10 inch painting will cost £6 for the mount and £26 for the frame, which is £32 total. We can calculate that each additional inch of mount and frame for a square painting costs £2.50; £2 for the frame and £0.50 for the mount. So an 11 inch painting will cost £34.50 to frame and mount, a 12 inch £37, a 13 inch £39.50, a 14 inch £42. The biggest painting that can be mounted and framed for £40 is a 13 inch painting.

Question 113: D
Recognise that the pattern is *"consonants move forward by two consonants; vowel stay the same"*. This allows coding of the word MAGICAL to PAJIFAN to RALIHAQ.

Forward two			Forward two
M	$\Rightarrow$	O (skips to) P	$\Rightarrow$ R
A	$\Rightarrow$	Stays the same	$\Rightarrow$ A
G	$\Rightarrow$	I (skips to) J	$\Rightarrow$ L
I	$\Rightarrow$	Stays the same	$\Rightarrow$ I
C	$\Rightarrow$	E (skips to) F	$\Rightarrow$ H
A	$\Rightarrow$	Stays the same	$\Rightarrow$ A
L	$\Rightarrow$	N	$\Rightarrow$ Q

Question 114: C
If f donates the flat rate, and k denotes the rate per km, we can form simultaneous equations:
f + 5k = £6 AND f + 3k = £4.20
Subtract equation two from equation one:
(f + 5k) - (f + 3k) = £6 - £4.20
Thus, 2k = £1.80 and k = £0.90
Therefore, f + (5 x 0.90) = £6
So, f + £4.50 = £6. Thus, f = £1.50
7k will be £1.50 + 7 x £0.90 = £7.80

Question 115: C

The increase from 2001/2 to 2011/12 was 1,019 to 11,736, which equals a linear increase of 10,717 admissions. So, in 20 years, we would expect to see an increase by 10,717 x 2 = 21,434. Add this to the number in 2011 to give 33,170 admissions.

Question 116: A

As the question uses percentages, it does not matter what figure you use. To make calculations easier, use an initial price of £100. When on sale, the dress is 20% off, so using a normal price of £100, the dress would be £80. When the dresses are 20% off, the shop is making a 25% profit. Therefore: £80 = 1.25 x purchase price.

Therefore, the purchase price is: $\frac{80}{1.25} = £64$. Thus, the normal profit is £100 - £64 = £36. I.e. when a dress sells for £100, the shop makes £36 or 36% profit.

Question 117: C

1. Incorrect. There must be 6 general committee clinical students, plus the treasurer, and 2 sabbatical roles, none of whom can be preclinical, so there must be a maximum of 11 preclinical students.
2. Correct. There must two general for each year plus welfare and social officers, totalling to 6.
3. Incorrect. The committee is made up of 20 students, 2 roles are sabbatical, so there are 18 studying students, and therefore there can be 3 from each year.
4. Correct. There are 18 studying students on the committee, and there must be 6 general committee members from pre-clinical, plus welfare and social, therefore there must be a minimum of 8 pre-clinical students, so there must be 10 clinical students.
5. Incorrect. You need to count up the number of specific roles on the committee, which is 5, and there must be 2 students from each year, which is 12. This leaves 3 more positions, which the question doesn't state can't be first years. Therefore there could be up to 5 first years.
6. Incorrect. There must be at least 2 general committee members from each year. However, the worked answer to 5 shows there are 15 general committee members which are split across the 6 years, and so there must be an uneven distribution.

Question 118: B

Remember 2012 was a leap year. Work through each month, adding the correct number of days, to work out what day each 13th would be on.

If a month was 28 days, the 13th would be the same day each month, therefore to work this out quickly, you only need to count on the number of days over 28. For example, in a month with 31 days, the 13th will be 3 weekdays (31-28) later.

Thus if 13th January is a Friday, 13th February is a Monday, (February has 29 days in 2012), 13th March is a Tuesday and 13th April is a Friday.

Question 119: E

There are 18 sheep in total. The question states there are 8 male sheep, which means there are 10 female sheep before some die. 5 female sheep die, so there are 5 female sheep alive to give birth to lambs. Each delivers 2 lambs, making 10 lambs in total. There are 4 male sheep and 5 mothers so the total is 10 + 4 + 5 = 19 sheep.

Question 120: D

We can see from the fact that all the possible answers end "AME" that the letters "AME" must be translated to the last 3 letters of the coded word, "JVN", under the code. J is the 10th letter of the alphabet so it is 9 letters on from A (V is the 21st letter of the alphabet and M is the 13th, and N is the 14th letter of the alphabet and E is the 5th, therefore these pairs are also 9 letters apart). Therefore P is the code for the letter 9 letters before it in the alphabet. P is the 16th letter of the alphabet, therefore it is the code for the 7th letter of the alphabet, G. Therefore from these solutions the only possibility for the original word is GAME.

Question 121: C

Let x be the number of people who get on the bus at the station.

It is easiest to work backwards. After the 4th stop, there are 5 people on the bus. At the 4th stop, half the people who were on the bus got off (and therefore half stayed on) and 2 people got on. Therefore, 5 is equal to 2 plus half the number of people who were on the bus after the 3rd stop. So half the number of people who were on the bus after the 3rd stop must be 3. Therefore, after the 3rd stop, there must have been 6 people on the bus.

We can then say that 6 is equal to 2 plus half the number of people who were on the bus after the 2nd stop. Therefore there were 8 people on the bus after the 2nd stop.

We can then say that 8 is equal to 2 plus half the number of people who were on the bus after the 1st stop. Therefore there were 12 people on the bus after the 1st stop.

We can then say that 12 is equal to 2 plus half the number of people who got on the bus at the station. Therefore the number of people who got on the bus at the station is 20.

Question 122: B

We know from the question that I have purchased small cans of blue and white paint, and that blue paint accounted for 50% of the total cost. Since a can of blue paint is 4 X the price of a can of white paint, we know I must have purchased 4 cans of white paint for each can of blue paint.

Each can of small paint covers a total of $10m^2$, and I have painted a total of $100m^2$, in doing so using up all the paint. Therefore, I must have purchased 10 cans of paint. Therefore, I must have purchased 2 cans of blue paint and 8 cans of white paint. So I must have painted $20m^2$ of wall space blue.

Question 123: E

The cost for x cakes under this offer can be expressed as: $x(42-x^2)$

Following this formula, we can see that 2 cakes would cost 76p, 3 cakes would cost 99p, and 4 cakes would cost 104p. As the number of cakes increases beyond 4, we see that the overall price actually drops, as 5 cakes would cost 85p and 6 cakes would cost 36p. This confirms Isobel's prediction that the offer is a bad deal for the baker, as it ends up cheaper for the customer to purchase more cakes. It is clear that 6 cakes is the smallest number for which the price will be under 40p, and the price will continue to drop as more cakes are purchased.

Question 124: C

Adding up the percentages of students in University A who do "Science" subjects gives:
$23.50 + 6.25 + 30.25 = 60\%$.
60% of 800 students is 480, so 480 students in University A do "Science" subjects.
Adding up the percentages of students in University B who do "Science subjects" gives:
$13.25 + 14.75 + 7.00 = 35\%$. 35% of 1200 students is 420, so 420 students in University B do "Science" subjects. Therefore:
$480 - 420 = 60$
60 more students in University A than University B take a "Science" subject.

Question 125: C

Let the number of miles Sonia is travelling be x. Because she is crossing 1 international border, travelling by Traveleasy Coaches will cost Sonia: £(5 + 0.5x)
Travelling by Europremier coaches will cost Sonia: £(15 + 0.1x).

Because we know the cost is the same for both companies, the number of miles she is travelling can be found by setting these two expressions equal to each other: $5 + 0.5x = 15 + 0.1x$.
This equation can be rearranged to give: $0.4x = 10$
Therefore: $x = 10/0.4 = 25$

Question 126: E

To find out whether many of these statements are true it is necessary to work out the departure and arrival times, and journey time, for each girl.

Lauren departs at 2:30pm and arrives at 4pm, therefore her journey takes 1.5 hours
Chloe departs at 1:30pm and her journey takes 1 hour longer than 1.5 hours (Lauren's journey), therefore her journey takes 2.5 hours and she arrives at 4pm
Amy arrives at 4:15pm and her journey takes 2 times 1.5 hours (Lauren's journey), therefore her journey takes 3 hours and she departs at 1:15pm.
Looking at each statement, the only one which is definitely true is **E**: Amy departs at 1:15pm and Chloe departs at 1:30pm therefore Amy departed before Chloe.

D *may* be true, but nothing in the question shows it is *definitely* true, so it can be safely ignored.

Question 127: B
First consider how many items of clothing she can take by weight. The weight allowance is 20kg. Take off 2kg for the weight of the empty suitcase, then take off another 3kg (3 X 1000g) for the books she wishes to take. Therefore she can fit 15kg of clothes in her suitcase. To find out how many items of clothing this is, we can divide 15kg=15000g by 400g: 15000/400 = 150/4 = 37.5
So she can pack up to 37 items of clothing by weight.

Now consider the volume of clothes she can fit in. The total volume of the suitcase is:
50cm x 50cm x 20cm = 50000cm³
The volume of each book is: 0.2m x 0.1m x 0.05m = 1000cm³

So the volume of space available for clothes is: 50000 – (3 x 1000) = 47000cm³
To find out how many items of clothing she can fit in this space, we can divide 47000 by 1500:
47000/1500 = 470/15 = 31 1/3
So she can pack up to 31 items of clothing by volume.

Although she can fit 37 items by weight, they will not fit in the volume of the suitcase, so the maximum number of items of clothing she can pack is 31.

Question 128: D
We can work out the Answer by considering each option:
Bed Shop A: £120 + £70 = £190
Bed Shop B: £90 + £90 = £180
Bed Shop C: £140 + (1/2 x £60) = £170
Bed Shop D: (2/3) x (£140+£100) = (2/3) x (£240) = £160
Bed Shop E: £175
Therefore the cheapest is Bed Shop **D**.

Question 129: C
The numbers of socks of each colour is irrelevant, so long as there is more than one of each (which there is). There are only 4 colours of socks, so if Joseph takes 5 socks, it is guaranteed that at least 2 of them will be the same colour.

Question 130: D
Paper comes in packs of 500, and with each pack 20 magazines can be printed. Each pack costs £3.
Card comes in packs of 60, and with each pack 60 magazines can be printed. Each pack costs £3 x 2 = £6.
Each ink cartridge prints 130 sheets, which is 130/26 = 5 magazines. Each cartridge costs £5.

The lowest common multiple of 20, 60 and 5 is 60, so it is possible to work out the total cost for printing 60 magazines. Printing 60 magazines will require 3 packs of paper at £3, 1 pack of card at £6 and 12 ink cartridges at £5. So the total cost of printing 60 magazines is: (3 x 3) + 6 + (12 x 5) = £75.

The total budget is £300.
£300/£75 = 4
So we can print 4x60 magazines in this budget, which is 240 magazines.

Question 131: E
We can express the information we have as: $\dfrac{1}{4} - \dfrac{1}{5} = \dfrac{1}{20}$
So the six additional lengths make up 1/20 of Rebecca's intended distance. So the number of lengths she intended to complete was: 20 x 6 = 120.

Question 132: B
Sammy has a choice of 3 flavours for the first sweet that he eats. Each of the other sweets he eats cannot be the same flavour as the sweet he has just eaten. So he has a choice of 2 flavours for each of these four sweets. So the total number of ways that he can make his choices is:
$3 \times 2 \times 2 \times 2 \times 2 = 48$

Question 133: C

Suppose that today Gill is x years old. It follows that Granny is $15x$ years old. In 4 years' time, Gill will be $(x+4)$ years old and Granny will be $15x+4$ years old. We know that in 4 years' time, Granny's age is equal to Gill's age squared, so: $15x + 4 = (x + 4)^2$

Expanding and rearranging, we get: $x^2 - 7x + 12 = 0$

We can factorise this to get: $(x - 3)(x - 4)$

So x is either 3 or 4. Gill's age today is either 3 or 4 so Granny is either 45 or 60. We know Granny's age is an even number, so she must be 60 and hence Gill must be 4. So the difference in their ages is 56 years.

Question 134: C

If Pierre is telling the truth, everyone else is not telling the truth. But, also in this case, what Qadr said is not true, and hence Ratna is telling the truth. So we have a contradiction. So we deduce that Pierre is not telling the truth. Therefore, Qadr is telling the truth, and so Ratna is not telling the truth. So Sven is also telling the truth, and hence Tanya is not telling the truth. So Qadr and Sven are telling the truth and the other three are not telling the truth.

Question 135: D

Angus walks for 20 minutes at 3 mph and runs for 20 minutes at 6 mph. 20 minutes is one-third of an hour. So the number of miles that Angus covers is: $3 \times \frac{1}{3} + 6 \times \frac{1}{3} = 6$

Bruce covers the same distance. So Bruce walks $\frac{1}{2} \times 3$ miles at 3 mph which takes him 30 minutes and runs the same distance at 6 mph which takes him 15 minutes. So altogether it takes Bruce 45 minutes to finish the course.

Question 136: B

Although you could do this quickly by forming simultaneous equations, it is even quicker to note that 72 x 4 = 288. Since Species 24601 each have 4 legs; it leaves a single member of species 8472 to account for the other 2 legs.

Question 137: E

None of the options can be concluded for certain. We are not told whether any chicken dishes are spicy, only that they are all creamy. Whilst all vegetable dishes are spicy, some non-vegetable dishes could also be spicy. There is no information on whether dishes can be both creamy and spicy, nor on which, if any, dishes contain tomatoes. Remember, if you're really stuck, draw a Venn diagram for these types of questions.

Question 138: C

At 10mph, we can express the time it takes Lucy to get home as: $60 \times 8/10 = 48$

Since Simon sets off 20 minutes later, his time taken to get home, in order to arrive at the same time, must be: $48 - 20 = 28$

Therefore his cycling speed must be: $48/28 \times 10 = 17$mph

Question 139: A

The total profit from the first transaction can be expressed as: $2000 \times 8 = 16,000$p

The total profit from the second transaction is: $1000 \times 6 = 6,000$p

Therefore the total profit is 22,000p or £220 before charges. There are four transactions at a cost of £20 each, therefore the overall profit is: £220 – (20 x 4) = £140

Question 140: C

For the total score to be odd, there must be either three odd or one odd and two even scores obtained. Since the solitary odd score could be either the first, second or third throw there are four possible outcomes that result in an odd total score. Additionally, there are the same number of possibilities giving an even score (either all three even or two odd and one even scores obtained), and the chance of throwing odd or even with any given dart is equal. Therefore, there is an equal probability of three darts totalling to an odd score as to an even score, and so the chance of an odd score is ½.

Question 141 C

This is a compound interest question. £5,000 must be increased by 5%, and then the answer needs to be increased by 5% for four more iterations. After one year: £5,000 x 1.05 = £5,250

Increasing sequentially gives 5512, 5788, 6077 and 6381 after five years. Therefore the answer is £6,381.

Question 142: D

If in 5 years' time the sum of their ages is 62, the sum of their ages today will be: 62 – (5 x 2) = 52

Therefore if they were the same age they would both be 26, but with a 12 year age gap they are 20 and 32 today. Michael is the older brother, so 2 years ago he would have been aged 30.

Question 143: A

Tearing out every page which is a multiple of 3 removes 166 pages. All multiples of 6 are multiples of 3, so no more pages are torn out with that instruction. Finally, half of the remaining pages are removed, which equates to an additional 167 pages. Therefore 333 pages are removed in total. The total surface area of these pages is 15 x 30 x 333 = 149,850 cm^2 = 14.9m^2. At 110 gm^2, 14.9 m^2 weighs 14.9 x 110 = 1,650g (1,648g unrounded)

Question 144: D

The cost of fertiliser is 80p/kg = 8p/100g. At 200g the incremental increase in yield is 65 pence/m. At each additional 100g it will be reduced by 30%, therefore at 300g/m it is 45.5p, at 400g/m it is 31.8p, at 500g/m it is 22.3p, at 600g/m it is 15.6p, at 700g/m it is 10.9p, and at 800g it is 7.6p. So at 800g the gain in yield is less than the cost of the fertiliser to produce the gain, and so it is no longer cost effective to fertilise more.

Question 145: D

Statements **A**, **C** and **E** are all definitely true. Meanwhile, statement **B** may be not true but is not definitely untrue, as this depends on the number of cats and rabbit owned.

Only statement **D** is definitely untrue. The type of animal requiring the most food is a dog, and as can be seen from the tables, Furry Friends actually sells the most expensive dog food, not the cheapest.

Question 146: C

The largest decrease in bank balance occurs between January 1st and February 1st, totalling £171, reflecting the amount spent during the month of January, £1171. However, because there is a pay rise beginning on March 10th, we need to consider that from April onwards, the bank balance will have increased by £1100, not £1000. This means that the same decrease in bank balance reflects £100 more spending if it occurs after March. This means that 2 months now have seen more spending than February. Between March 1st and April 1st, the bank balance has decreased by £139. With the salary increase, the salary is now £1100, so the total spending for the month of March is £1239. This is greater than the total spending during the month of January.

Similarly, the month of April has also seen more spending than January once the pay rise is considered, a total of £1225 of spending. However, this is still less than the month of March.

Question 147: C

If Amy gets a taxi, she can set off 100 minutes before 1700, which is 1520.

If Amy gets a train, she must get the 1500 train as the later train arrives after 1700, so she must set off at 1500.

Since Northtown airport is 30 minutes from Northtown station, there is no way Amy can get the flight and still arrive at Northtown station by 1700. Therefore Amy should get a taxi and should leave at 1520.

Question 148: C

We can decompose the elements of the multiplication grid into their prime factors, thus:

	C	D
A	2 x 2 x 2 x 3 x 7	2 x 2 x 2 x 2 x 3 x 3 x 5
B	7 x 17	2 x 3 x 5 x 17

bc = 7 x 17, so one of b and c must be 7 and the other must be 17. b must be 17 because bd is a multiple of 17 and not of 7, and c must be 7 because ac is a multiple of 7 and not of 17. ac is 168, so a must be 168 divided by 7, which is 24. ad is 720 so d must be 720 divided by 24, which is 30. Hence the answer is 30.

Alternatively approach the question by eliminating all answers which are not factors of both 720 and 510.

Question 149: E

48% of the students are girls, which is 720 students. Hence 80 is 1/9 of the girls, so 1/9 of boys are mixed race. The remaining 780 students are boys, so 87 boys are mixed race to the nearest person. There is a shortcut to this question. Notice that 80 girls are mixed race, and the proportion is the same for boys. As there are more boys than girls we know the answer is greater than 80. Option **E** 90 is the only option for which this holds true.

Question 150: D

Don't be fooled – this is surprisingly easy. We can see that between Monday and Thursday, Christine has worked a total of 30 hours. We can also calculate how long her shift on Friday was supposed to be. She is able to make up the hours by working 3 extra hours next week, and 5 hours on Sunday. Thus, the Friday shift must have been planned to be 8 hours long. Adding this to the other 30 hours, we see that Christine was supposed to work 38 hours this week.

Question 151: C

130°. Each hour is 1/12 of a complete turn, equalling 30°. The smaller angle between 8 and 12 on the clock face is 4 gaps, therefore 120°. In addition, there is 1/3 of the distance between 3 and 4 still to turn, so an additional 10° must be added on to account for that.

Question 152: B

The total price of all of these items would usually be £17. However, with the DVD offer, the customer saves £1, giving a total cost of £16. Thus, the customer will need to receive £34 in change.

Question 153: E

A. Incorrect. UCL study found eating more portions of fruit and vegetables was beneficial.
B. Incorrect. This is a possible reason but has yet to be fully investigated.
C. Incorrect. Fruit and vegetables are more protective against cardiovascular disease, and were shown to have little effect on cancer rates.
D. Incorrect. Inconclusive – people who ate more vegetables generally had a lower mortality but unknown if this is due to eating more vegetables or other associated factors.
E. Correct. Although this has previously been the case, this study did not find so. 'they recorded no additional decline for people who ate over 5 portions'.
F. Incorrect. The 5% decline per portion was only up to 5 portions and no additional reduction in mortality for 7 than 5 portions.
G. Incorrect. Study only looks at cancers in general and states need to look into specific cancers.

Question 154: C

Deaths in meta-analysis = 56423/800000 = 0.07 or 7%
1% lower in UCL study so 6%
6% of 65,000 = 65000 x 0.06 = 3,900

Question 155: B

A. Eating more fruit and vegetables doesn't particularly lower overall risk but need research into specific cancer risk.
B. The UCL research alone found that increasing the number of fruit and vegetable portions had a beneficial effect, even though this wasn't the overall conclusion when combined with results from the meta-analysis.
C. The results were not exactly the same but showed similar overall trends.
D. Although this may be true, there is no mention of this in the passage.
E. Fruit and vegetables are protective against cardiovascular disease, but not exclusively. They also reduce the rates of death from all causes.
F. The UCL study is in England only and the meta-analysis a combination of studies from around the world.
G. Suggested by the UCL research, but not the meta-analysis, so not an overall conclusion of the article.

Question 156: E

Remember that you don't need to calculate exact values for question 249 – 251. Thus, you should round numbers frequently to make this more manageable. Work out percentage of beer and wine consumption and then the actual value using the total alcohol consumption figure:

Belarus: 17.3 + 5.2 = 22.5%;
0.225 x 17.5 = 3.94

Lithuania: Missing figure 100 – 7.8 – 34.1 – 11.6 = 46.5
46.5 + 7.8 = 54.3%
0.543 x 15.4 = 8.36

France: 18.8 + 56.4 = 75.2%
0.752 x 12.2 = 9.17

Ireland: 48.1 + 26.1 = 74.2
0.742 x 11.9 = 8.83

Andorra: missing figure 100 – 34.6 – 20.1 = 45.3
34.6 + 45.3 = 79.9%
0.799 x 13.8 = 11.0

Question 157: D

Russia:
2010 – Total = 11.5+3.6 = 15.1. Spirits = 0.51 x 15.1 = 7.7
2020 – Total = 14.5. Spirits = 0.51 x 14.5 = 7.4
Difference = 0.3 L

Belarus:
2010 – Total = 14.4 + 3.2 = 17.6. Spirits = 0.466 x 17.6 = 8.2
2020 – Total = 17.1. Spirits = 0.466 x 17.1 = 8.0
Difference = 0.2 L

Lithuania:
2010 – Total = 15.4. Spirits = 0.341 x 15.4 = 5.3
2020 – Total = 16.2. Spirits = 0.341 x 16.2 = 5.5
Difference = 0.2 L

Grenada:
2010 – Total = 12.5. Spirits % = 100 – 29.3 – 4.3 – 0.2 = 66.2%. Spirits = 0.662 x 12.5 = 8.3
2020 – Total = 10.4. Spirits = 0.662 x 10.4 = 6.8
Difference = 1.5 L

Ireland:
2010 – Total = 11.9. Spirits = 0.187 x 11.9 = 2.2
2020 – Total = 10.9. Spirits = 0.187 x 10.9 = 2
Difference = 0.2 L

Question 158: C

Work out 4.9 as a percentage of total beer consumption in Czech Republic and search other rows for similar percentage.

4.9/13 = 0.38, approx. 38% which is very similar to percentage consumption in Russia (37.6).

Question 189: B

We can add up the total incidence of the 6 cancers in men, which is 94,000. Then we can add up the total incidence in women, which is 101,000. As a percentage of 10 million, this is 0.94% of men and 1.01% of women. Therefore the difference is 0.07%.

Question 160: C
Given there are 1.15 times as many men as women, the incidence of each cancer amongst men needs to be greater than 1.15 times the incidence amongst women in order for a man to be more likely to develop it. The incidence is at least 1.15 higher in men for 3 cancers (prostate, lung and bladder).

Question 161: D
If 10% of cancer patients are in Sydney, there are 10,300 prostate/bladder/breast cancer patients and 9,200 lung/bowel/uterus cancer patients in Sydney. Hence the total number of hospital visits is 10,300 + 18,400, which is 28,700.

Question 162: A
The proportion of men with bladder cancer is 2/3 and women 1/3.

Question 163: D
First we work out the size of each standard drink. 50 standard drinks of vodka is equivalent to 1250ml, so one drink is 25ml or 0.025 litres. 11.4 standard drinks of beer is 10 pints of 5700ml, so one standard drink is 500ml or 0.5 litres. 3 standard drinks of cocktail is 750ml so one is 250ml or 0.25 litres. 3.75 standard drinks of wine is 750ml, so one is 200ml or 0.2 litres.
We can then work out the number of units in each drink. Vodka has 0.025 x 40 = 1 unit, Beer has 0.5 x 3 = 1.5 units, Cocktail has 0.25 x 8 = 2 units and Wine has 0.2 x 12.5 = 2.5 units. Since the drink with the most units is wine, the answer is D.

Question 164: B
We found in the last question that vodka has 1 unit, beer has 1.5, cocktail has 2 and wine has 2.5. Hence in the week, Hannah drinks 23.5 units and Mark drinks 29 units. Hence Hannah exceeds the recommended amount by 9.5 units and Mark by 9 units.

Question 165: D
We found that vodka has 1 unit, beer has 1.5, cocktail has 2 and wine has 2.5. Hence it is possible to make 5 combinations of drinks that are 4 units: 4 vodkas, 2 cocktails, 2 vodkas and a cocktail, 1 vodka and 2 beers, or a wine and a beer.

Question 166: D
The total number of males in Greentown is 12,890. Adding up the rest of the age categories, we can see that 10,140 of these are in the older age categories. Hence there are 2750 males under 20.

Question 167: C
Given that in the first question we found the number of males under 20 is 2,750, we can then add up the totals in the age categories (apart from 40-59) in order to find that 15,000 of the residents of Greentown are in other age categories. Hence 9,320 of the population are aged 40-59. We know that 4,130 of these are male, therefore 5,190 must be female.

Question 168: C
The age group with the highest ratio of males:females is 20-39, with approximately 1.9 males per females (approximately 3800:2000). As a ratio of females to males, this is 1:1.9.

Question 169: C
There are 4 instances where the line for Newcastle is flat from one month to the next per year, hence in 2008-2012 (5 years) there are 20 occasions when the average temperature is the same from month to month. During 2007, there are 2 occasions, and during 2013 there are 3.

Question 170: A
The average temperature is lower than the previous month in London for all months from August to December, which is 5 months. However, in August and November in Newcastle, the average temperature remains the same as the previous month. Hence there are only 3 months where the average temperature is lower in both cities. Hence from 2007 to 2012, there are 18 months where the average temperature is lower than the previous month. During 2013, the only included month where the temperature is lower in both cities than the previous month is September. Hence there are 19 months in total when the temperature is lower in both cities than the previous month.

Question 171: B
Firstly work out the difference between average temperatures for each month (2, 3, 1, 2, 1, 3, 3, 2, 2, 5, 1, 0). Then sum them to give 25. Divide by the number of months (12) to give $2^1/_{12}$, which is 2°C to the nearest 0.5°C.

Question 172: D
There is not enough information to tell which month the highest sales are in. We know it increases up to a point and decreases after it, but as we don't know by how much we cannot project where the maximum sales will be.

Question 173: B
Given that by observation, Q2 and Q3 both account for 1/3 of the sales and Q4 accounts for 1/4, this leaves that Q1 accounts for 1/12 of sales. 1/12 of £354,720 is £29,560.

Question 174: A
Quarter 2 accounts for 1/3 of the sales, which is £60,000 in sales revenue. If a tub of ice cream is sold for £2 and costs the manufacturer £1.50, this means profit is 1/4 of sales revenue. Hence £15,000 profit is made during Q2. Hence the answer is A.

Question 175: D
A. and B – Incorrect. Both *could* be true but neither is *definitely* true as it is dependent on the relative number of families with each number of children, which is not given in the question. Therefore we cannot know for certain whether these statements are true.
C – Incorrect. C is definitely *untrue* as half of the families spend £400 a month on food, which totals £4800 a year.
D – Correct. This option is true as 1/6 of families with 1 child and 1/6 of families with 3 children spent £100 a month on food.
E – Incorrect. This option is definitely untrue as the average expenditure for families with 2 children is actually £400 a month.

Question 176: B
2210 out of 2500 filled in responses, meaning that 290 did not. 290 as a percentage of 2500 is roughly 12% (11.6%) of the school that did not respond.

Question 177: C
The percentage of students that saw bullying and reported it was 35%, so 65% of those who saw it did not which is equivalent to 725 students. Of this 725, 146 which roughly equals 20%, gave the reason that they did not think it was important.

Question 178: B
Of the students who told a teacher, 286 did not witness any action. Of those who did notice action, i.e. 110, only 40% noticed any direct action with the bully involved. 40% of 110 is 44, so the correct answer is B.

Question 179: D
"427 cited fears of being found out" which means about 59% out of the 725 students that did not tell about the bullying, cited that it was because they worried about others finding out.

Question 180: F
North-east: 56 per 100,000 on average. This means that there must be a higher proportion of women than this and a lower proportion of men, such that the average is 56/100,000
We must make the reasonable assumption that there are the same number of men and women in the population as the question asks us to approximate.
Therefore there are 18.6/50,000 men and 37.3/50,000 women
This scales to 74.4/100,000 women which is roughly 74/100,000.

Question 181: C
8 million children – question tells to approximate to 4 million girls and 4 million boys.
Girls: 20% eat 5 portions fruit and vegetables a day. 20% of 4 million: 4 x 0.2 = 0.8 million
Boys: 16% eat 5 portions of fruit and vegetables a day. 16% of 4 million: 4 x 0.16 = 0.64 million
Number of more girls: 800,000 – 640,000 = 160,000.

Question 182: B
A. Incorrect. Women: 13619+10144+6569 = 30332. Men: 16818 + 9726 + 7669 + 6311 = 40524
B. Correct. Flu + pneumonia, lung cancer and chronic lower respiratory diseases = 15361 + 13619 + 14927 = 43907
C. Incorrect. More common cause of death but no information surrounding prevalence.
D. Incorrect. Colon cancer ranking 8 for both.

Question 183: A
The government has claimed a 20% reduction, so we are looking for an assessment criterion which has reduced 20% from 2013 to 2014. We can see that only "Number of people waiting for over 4 hours in A&E" has reduced by 20%, so this must be the criterion the government has used to describe "waiting times in A&E". Thus, the answer is A.

Question 184: B
Rovers must have played 10 games overall as they played each other's team twice. They lost 9 games scoring no points and so must have won 1 game, which scores 3 points.

Question 185: A
To have finished between City and United, Athletic must have got between 23 and 25 points. Hence they must have got 24 points because no team got the same number of points as another. Athletic won 7 games which is 21 points, so they must have also got 3 points from drawing 3 games. This accounts for all 10 games they played, so they did not lose any games.

Question 186: C
United won 8 games and drew 1, which is 25 points. Rangers drew 2 games and won none, which is 2 points. Therefore the difference in points is 23.

Question 187: C
Type 1 departments reached the new target of 95% at least three times since it was introduced. All the other statements are correct.

Question 188: C
Total attendances in Q1 08-9: 5.0 million
Total attendances in Q1 04-5: 4.5 million
The difference = 0.5 million
0.5/5 x 100 = 10% increase

Question 189: C
There are 16 quarters in total since the new target came into effect.
4/16 = 0.25, so the target has been hit 25% of the time i.e. missed 75% of the time.

Question 190: C
Ranjna must leave Singapore by 20:00 to get to Bali by 22:00. The latest flight she can therefore get is the 19:00. Thus, she must arrive in Singapore by 17:00 (accounting 2 hours for the stopover). The flight from Manchester to Singapore takes 14 hours. Manchester is 8 hours behind Singapore so she must leave Manchester 22 hours before 17:00 on Wednesday i.e. by 19:00 on Wednesday. Thus, the latest flight she can get is the 18:00 on Wednesday.

Question 191: D
The 08:00 flight will arrive at Singapore for 22:00 on Monday (GMT) or 06:00 Tuesday Singapore time. She then needs a 2 hour stopover, so earliest connecting flight she can get is 08:30 on Tuesday. The flight lands in Bali at 10:30. She then spends 1 hour and 45 minutes getting to her destination – arriving at 12:15 Tuesday.

Question 192: C
A. Incorrect. The graph is about level, and certainly not the steepest gradient post 2007.
B. Incorrect. Although there has been a general decline, there are some blips of increased smoking.
C. Correct.
D. Incorrect. The smoking rate in men decreased from 51% in 1974 to 21% in 2010. Thus, it decreased by more than a half.
E. Incorrect. The percentage difference between men and women smokers has been minimal in the 21st century.

Question 193: D
For this type of question you will have to use trial and error after you've analysed the data pattern to find the correct answer. The quickest way to do this is to examine outliers to try and match them to data in the table e.g. the left-most point is an outlier for the X-axis but average for the y-axis. Also look for any duplicated results in the table and if they are present on the graph, e.g. Hannah and Alice weigh 68 kg but this can't be found on the graph.

Question 194: C
This is pretty straightforward; the point is at approximately 172-174 cm in height and 164 -166 cm in arm span. Matthew is the only student who fits these dimensions.

Question 195: C
This is straightforward – just label the diagram using the information in the text and it becomes obvious that C is the correct answer.

Question 196: C
Since we do not know whether they went to university or not, we must add the number of women with children who work and those who went to university, 2, to the number of women with children who work but did not go to university, 1 (2 + 1 = 3).

Question 197: C
To work this out we must add up all the numbers within the rectangle, 4 + 6 + 1 + 2 + 11 + 12 + 7 + 15 = 58

Question 198: E
Calculate the number of men + women who have children and work i.e. 11 + 5 + 2 = 18

Question 199: C
To solve this we must work out the total number of people who had children i.e. 3 + 6 + 5 + 11 + 1 + 2 = 28. Then we work out the total number of people who went to university, but that do not also have children so that these are not counted twice: 13 + 12 = 25. Then we add these two numbers together, 28 + 25 = 53 and subtract the number of people who fell into both categories i.e. 53 - (5 + 11 + 2) = 35

Question 200: C
To work this out we must add up all the numbers outside the rectangle that also fall within both the circle and the square, which is 5.

Question 201: D & E
This question asks for identification of the blank space, which is the space within the triangle, the rectangle and the square i.e. indicating working women who went to university but did not have children. This also reveals non-working men who did not have children and did not go to university.

Question 202: C
The normal price of these items would be £18.50 (£8 + £7 + £3.50). However, with the 50% discount on meat products, the price in the sale for these items will be £9.25. Thus, Alfred would receive £10.75 of change from a £20 note.

Question 203: C
The number of games played and points scored is a red herring in this question. The important data is 'Goals For' and 'Goals Against'. As this is a defined league and the teams have only played each other, the 'Goals For' column must equal the 'Goals Against' column.
Total Goals For = 16 + 11 + 8 + 7 + 8 + 4 = 54
Total Goals Against = 2 + Wilmslow + 7 + 9 + 12 + 14 = 44 + Wilmslow
For both columns to be equal, Wilmslow must have a total of 54 – 44 = 10 Goals Against.

Question 204: C
Working with the table it is possible to work out that the BMIs of Julie and Lydia must be 21 and 23, and hence their weights 100 and 115 lbs. Thus Emma's weight is 120 lbs, and her BMI must be 22, making her height equivalent to 160 cm.

Question 205: C
Working through the results, starting with the highest and lowest values, it is possible to plot all values and decipher which point is marked.

Question 206: D
This is a question of estimation. The average production across the year is at least 7 million barrels per day. Multiplying this by 365 gives around 2,550 million barrels per year. All other options require less than 7 million barrels daily production to be produced, and it is clear there is at least 7 million barrels per day. Therefore the answer is 2,700 million.

Alternatively we can estimate using 30 days per month, and multiplying the amount of barrels produced per day in each month by 30 (this is more accurate but more time consuming). 6+7+7+7.5+7.5+7+7.5+8+8.5+8.5+8+9 = 91.5, multiplying by 30 gives just over 2,700 million barrels.

Question 207: C
Use both graphs. For July, multiply the oil price by the amount sold in the month, and multiply by the number of days in the month. Thus, July = 7.5 million barrels x $75 per barrel x 31 days = $17,400 million = $17.4 billion

Question 208: B

Each three-block combination is mutually exclusive to any other combination, so the probabilities are added.

Each block pick is independent of all other picks, so the probabilities can be multiplied. For this scenario there are three possible combinations:

P(2 red blocks and 1 yellow block) = P(red then red then yellow) + P(red then yellow then red) + P(yellow then red then red) =

$$(\frac{12}{20} x \frac{11}{19} x \frac{8}{18}) + (\frac{12}{20} x \frac{8}{19} x \frac{11}{18}) + (\frac{8}{20} x \frac{12}{19} x \frac{11}{18}) =$$

$$\frac{3 \, x \, 12 \, x \, 11 \, x \, 8}{20 \, x \, 19 \, x \, 18} = \frac{44}{95}$$

Question 209: C

Multiply through by 15: $3(3x + 5) + 5(2x - 2) = 18 \, x \, 15$

Thus: $9x + 15 + 10x - 10 = 270$

$9x + 10x = 270 - 15 + 10$

$19x = 265$

$x = 13.95$

Question 210: C

This is a rare case where you need to factorise a complex polynomial:

(3x   )(x   ) = 0, possible pairs: 2 x 10, 10 x 2, 4 x 5, 5 x 4

(3x - 4)(x + 5) = 0

3x - 4 = 0, so x = $\frac{4}{3}$

x + 5 = 0, so x = -5

Question 211: C

$$\frac{5(x-4)}{(x+2)(x-4)} + \frac{3\,(x+2)}{(x+2)(x-4)}$$

$$= \frac{5x - 20 + 3x + 6}{(x + 2)(x - 4)}$$

$$= \frac{8x - 14}{(x + 2)(x - 4)}$$

Question 212: E

p α $\sqrt[3]{q}$, so p = k $\sqrt[3]{q}$

p = 12 when q = 27 gives 12 = k $\sqrt[3]{27}$, so 12 = 3k and k = 4

so p = 4 $\sqrt[3]{q}$

Now p = 24:

24 = 4$\sqrt[3]{q}$, so 6 = $\sqrt[3]{q}$ and q = 6^3 = 216

Question 213: A

8 x 9 = 72

8 = (4 x 2) = 2 x 2 x 2

9 = 3 x 3

(2 x 2 x 2 x 3 x 3)² = 2 x 2 x 2 x 2 x 2 x 2 x 3 x 3 x 3 x 3 = 2^6 x 3^4

Question 214: C

Note that 1.151 x 2 = 2.302.

Thus: $\dfrac{2 \times 10^5 + 2 \times 10^2}{10^{10}} = 2 \times 10^{-5} + 2 \times 10^{-8}$

= 0.00002 + 0.00000002 = 0.00002002

Question 215: E

y² + ay + b

= (y +2)² - 5 = y² + 4y + 4 - 5

= y² + 4y + 4 - 5 = y² + 4y - 1

So a = 4 and y = -1

Question 216: E

Take $5(m + 4n)$ as a common factor to give: $\dfrac{4(m + 4n)}{5(m + 4n)} + \dfrac{5(m - 2n)}{5(m + 4n)}$

Simplify to give: $\dfrac{4m + 16n + 5m - 10n}{5(m + 4n)} = \dfrac{9m + 6n}{5(m + 4n)} = \dfrac{3(3m + 2n)}{5(m + 4n)}$

Question 217: C

$A \, \alpha \dfrac{1}{\sqrt{B}}$. Thus, $= \dfrac{k}{\sqrt{B}}$.

Substitute the values in to give: $4 = \dfrac{k}{\sqrt{25}}$.

Thus, $k = 20$.

Therefore, $A = \dfrac{20}{\sqrt{B}}$.

When B = 16, $A = \dfrac{20}{\sqrt{16}} = \dfrac{20}{4} = 5$

Question 218: E

Angles SVU and STU are opposites and add up to 180°, so STU = 91°

The angle of the centre of a circle is twice the angle at the circumference so SOU = 2 x 91° = 182°

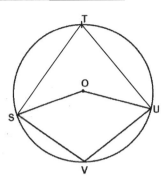

Question 219: E

The surface area of an open cylinder A = 2πrh. Cylinder B is an enlargement of A, so the increases in radius (r) and height (h) will be proportional: $\dfrac{r_A}{r_B} = \dfrac{h_A}{h_B}$. Let us call the proportion coefficient n, where n = $\dfrac{r_A}{r_B} = \dfrac{h_A}{h_B}$.

So $\dfrac{Area\ A}{Area\ B} = \dfrac{2\pi r_A h_A}{2\pi r_B h_B} = n \times n = n^2$ $\dfrac{Area\ A}{Area\ B} = \dfrac{32\pi}{8\pi} = 4$, so n = 2.

The proportion coefficient n = 2 also applies to their volumes, where the third dimension (also radius, i.e. the r^2 in V = πr²h) is equally subject to this constant of proportionality. The cylinder's volumes are related by $n^3 = 8$.

If the smaller cylinder has volume 2π cm³, then the larger will have volume 2π x n^3 = 2π x 8 = 16π cm³.

Question 220: E

$$= \frac{8}{x(3-x)} - \frac{6(3-x)}{x(3-x)}$$

$$= \frac{8 - 18 + 6x}{x(3-x)}$$

$$= \frac{6x - 10}{x(3-x)}$$

Question 221: B

For the black ball to be drawn in the last round, white balls must be drawn every round. Thus the probability is given by $P = \dfrac{9}{10} \times \dfrac{8}{9} \times \dfrac{7}{8} \times \dfrac{6}{7} \times \dfrac{5}{6} \times \dfrac{4}{5} \times \dfrac{3}{4} \times \dfrac{2}{3} \times \dfrac{1}{2}$

$= \dfrac{9 \times 8 \times 7 \times 6 \times 5 \times 4 \times 3 \times 2 \times 1}{10 \times 9 \times 8 \times 7 \times 6 \times 5 \times 4 \times 3 \times 2 \times 1} = \dfrac{1}{10}$

Question 222: C

The probability of getting a king the first time is $\dfrac{4}{52} = \dfrac{1}{13}$, and the probability of getting a king the second time is $\dfrac{3}{51}$. These are independent events, thus, the probability of drawing two kings is $\dfrac{1}{13} \times \dfrac{3}{51} = \dfrac{3}{663} = \dfrac{1}{221}$

Question 223: B

The probabilities of all outcomes must sum to one, so if the probability of rolling a 1 is x, then: $x + x + x + x + 2x = 1$. Therefore, $x = \dfrac{1}{7}$.

The probability of obtaining two sixes $P_{12} = \frac{2}{7} x \frac{2}{7} = \frac{4}{49}$

Question 224: B

There are plenty of ways of counting, however the easiest is as follows: 0 is divisible by both 2 and 3. Half of the numbers from 1 to 36 are even (i.e. 18 of them). 3, 9, 15, 21, 27, 33 are the only numbers divisible by 3 that we've missed. There are 25 outcomes divisible by 2 or 3, out of 37.

Question 225: C

List the six ways of achieving this outcome: HHTT, HTHT, HTTH, TTHH, THTH and THHT. There are 2^4 possible outcomes for 4 consecutive coin flips, so the probability of two heads and two tails is: $6 x \frac{1}{2^4} = \frac{6}{16} = \frac{3}{8}$

Question 226: D

Count the number of ways to get a 5, 6 or 7 (draw the square if helpful). The ways to get a 5 are: 1, 4; 2, 3; 3, 2; 4, 1. The ways to get a 6 are: 1, 5; 2, 4; 3, 3; 4, 2; 5, 1. The ways to get a 7 are: 1, 6; 2, 5; 3, 4; 4, 3; 5, 2; 6, 1. That is 15 out of 36 possible outcomes.

	1	2	3	4	5	6
1	2	3	4	5	6	7
2	3	4	5	6	7	8
3	4	5	6	7	8	9
4	5	6	7	8	9	10
5	6	7	8	9	10	11
6	7	8	9	10	11	12

Question 227: C

There are x+y+z balls in the bag, and the probability of picking a red ball is $\frac{x}{(x + y + z)}$ and the probability of picking a green ball is $\frac{z}{(x + y + z)}$. These are independent events, so the probability of picking red then green is $\frac{xz}{(x + y + z)^2}$ and the probability of picking green then red is the same. These outcomes are mutually exclusive, so are added.

Question 228: B

There are two ways of doing it, pulling out a red ball then a blue ball, or pulling out a blue ball and then a red ball. Let us work out the probability of the first: $\frac{x}{(x + y + z)} \times \frac{y}{x + y + z - 1}$, and the probability of the second option will be the same. These are mutually exclusive options, so the probabilities may be summed.

Question 229: A

[x: Player 1 wins point, y: Player 2 wins point]

Player 1 wins in five rounds if we get: yxxxx, xyxxx, xxyxx, xxxyx.

(Note the case of xxxxy would lead to player 1 winning in 4 rounds, which the question forbids.)

Each of these have a probability of $p^4(1-p)$. Thus, the solution is $4p^4(1-p)$.

Question 230: F

$4x + 7 + 18x + 20 = 14$

$22x + 27 = 14$

Thus, $22x = -13$

Giving $x = -\dfrac{13}{22}$

Question 231: D

$$r^3 = \frac{3V}{4\pi}$$

Thus, $r = \left(\dfrac{3V}{4\pi}\right)^{1/3}$

Therefore, S $= 4\pi\left[\left(\dfrac{3V}{4\pi}\right)^{\frac{1}{3}}\right]^2 = 4\pi\left(\dfrac{3V}{4\pi}\right)^{\frac{2}{3}}$

$$= \frac{4\pi(3V)^{\frac{2}{3}}}{(4\pi)^{\frac{2}{3}}} = (3V)^{\frac{2}{3}} \times \frac{(4\pi)^1}{(4\pi)^{\frac{2}{3}}}$$

$$= (3V)^{\frac{2}{3}}(4\pi)^{1-\frac{2}{3}} = (4\pi)^{\frac{1}{3}}(3V)^{\frac{2}{3}}$$

Question 232: A

Let each unit length be x.

Thus, $S = 6x^2$. Therefore, $x = \left(\dfrac{S}{6}\right)^{\frac{1}{2}}$

$V = x^3$. Thus, $V = \left[\left(\dfrac{S}{6}\right)^{\frac{1}{2}}\right]^3$ so $V = \left(\dfrac{S}{6}\right)^{\frac{3}{2}}$

Question 233: B

Multiplying the second equation by 2 we get 4x + 16y = 24. Subtracting the first equation from this we get 13y = 17, so y = $\dfrac{17}{13}$. Then solving for x we get x = $\dfrac{10}{13}$. You could also try substituting possible solutions one by one, although given that the equations are both linear and contain easy numbers, it is quicker to solve them algebraically.

Question 234: A

Multiply by the denominator to give: $(7x + 10) = (3y^2 + 2)(9x + 5)$

Partially expand brackets on right side: $(7x + 10) = 9x(3y^2 + 2) + 5(3y^2 + 2)$

Take x terms across to left side: $7x - 9x(3y^2 + 2) = 5(3y^2 + 2) - 10$

Take x outside the brackets: $x[7 - 9(3y^2 + 2)] = 5(3y^2 + 2) - 10$

Thus: $x = \dfrac{5(3y^2 + 2) - 10}{7 - 9(3y^2 + 2)}$

Simplify to give: $x = \dfrac{(15y^2)}{(7 - 9(3y^2 + 2))}$

Question 235: F

$$3x\left(\frac{3x^7}{x^{\frac{1}{3}}}\right)^3 = 3x\left(\frac{3^3x^{21}}{x^{\frac{3}{3}}}\right)$$

$$= 3x\frac{27x^{21}}{x} = 81x^{21}$$

Question 236: D

$$2x[2^{\frac{7}{14}}x^{\frac{7}{14}}] = 2x[2^{\frac{1}{2}}x^{\frac{1}{2}}]$$

$$= 2x(\sqrt{2}\sqrt{x}) = 2\left[\sqrt{x}\sqrt{x}\right]\left[\sqrt{2}\sqrt{x}\right]$$

$$= 2\sqrt{2x^3}$$

Question 237: A

$A = \pi r^2$, therefore $10\pi = \pi r^2$

Thus, $r = \sqrt{10}$

Therefore, the circumference is $2\pi\sqrt{10}$

Question 238: D

$3.4 = 12 + (3 + 4) = 19$

$19.5 = 95 + (19 + 5) = 119$

Question 239: D

$2.3 = \dfrac{2^3}{2} = 4$

$4.2 = \dfrac{4^2}{4} = 4$

Question 240: F

This is a tricky question that requires you to know how to 'complete the square':

$(x + 1.5)(x + 1.5) = x^2 + 3x + 2.25$

Thus, $(x + 1.5)^2 - 7.25 = x^2 + 3x - 5 = 0$

Therefore, $(x + 1.5)^2 = 7.25 = \dfrac{29}{4}$

Thus, $x + 1.5 = \sqrt{\dfrac{29}{4}}$

Thus $x = -\dfrac{3}{2} \pm \sqrt{\dfrac{29}{4}} = -\dfrac{3}{2} \pm \dfrac{\sqrt{29}}{2}$

Question 241: B

Whilst you definitely need to solve this graphically, it is necessary to complete the square for the first equation to allow you to draw it more easily:

$(x + 2)^2 = x^2 + 4x + 4$

Thus, $y = (x + 2)^2 + 10 = x^2 + 4x + 14$

This is now an easy curve to draw ($y = x^2$ that has moved 2 units left and 10 units up). The turning point of this quadratic is to the left and well above anything in x^3, so the only solution is the first intersection of the two curves in the upper right quadrant around (3.4, 39).

Question 242: C

The easiest way to solve this is to sketch them (don't waste time solving them algebraically). As soon as you've done this, it'll be very obvious that $y = 2$ and $y = 1 - x^2$ don't intersect, since the latter has its turning point at (0, 1) and zero points at $x = -1$ and 1. $y = x$ and $y = x^2$ intersect at the origin and (1, 1), and $y = 2$ runs through both.

Question 243: B

Notice that you're not required to get the actual values – just the number's magnitude. Thus, 897653 can be approximated to 900,000 and 0.009764 to 0.01. Therefore, 900,000 x 0.01 = 9,000

Question 244: C

Multiply through by 70: $7(7x + 3) + 10(3x + 1) = 14 \times 70$

Simplify: $49x + 21 + 30x + 10 = 980$

$79x + 31 = 980$

$$x = \frac{949}{79}$$

Question 245: A

Split the equilateral triangle into 2 right-angled triangles and apply Pythagoras' theorem:

$$x^2 = \left(\frac{x}{2}\right)^2 + h^2 \quad . \text{ Thus } \quad h^2 = \frac{3}{4}x^2$$

$$h = \sqrt{\frac{3x^2}{4}} = \frac{\sqrt{3x^2}}{2}$$

The area of a triangle = ½ x base x height = $\frac{1}{2}x\frac{\sqrt{3x^2}}{2}$

Simplifying gives: $x\frac{\sqrt{3x^2}}{4} = \frac{\sqrt{3}\sqrt{x^2}}{4} = \frac{x^2\sqrt{3}}{4}$

Question 246: A

This is a question testing your ability to spot 'the difference between two squares'.

Factorise to give: $3 - \dfrac{7x(5x - 1)(5x + 1)}{(7x)^2(5x + 1)}$

Cancel out: $3 - \dfrac{(5x - 1)}{7x}$

Question 247: C

The easiest way to do this is to 'complete the square':

$(x - 5)^2 = x^2 - 10x + 25$

Thus, $(x - 5)^2 - 125 = x^2 - 10x - 100 = 0$

Therefore, $(x - 5)^2 = 125$

$x - 5 = \pm\sqrt{125} = \pm\sqrt{25}\sqrt{5} = \pm 5\sqrt{5}$

$x = 5 \pm 5\sqrt{5}$

Question 248: B

Factorise by completing the square:

$x^2 - 4x + 7 = (x - 2)^2 + 3$

Simplify: $(x - 2)^2 = y^3 + 2 - 3$

$x - 2 = \pm\sqrt{y^3 - 1}$

$x = 2 \pm\sqrt{y^3 - 1}$

Question 249: D

Square both sides to give: $(3x + 2)^2 = 7x^2 + 2x + y$

Thus: $y = (3x + 2)^2 - 7x^2 - 2x = (9x^2 + 12x + 4) - 7x^2 - 2x$

$y = 2x^2 + 10x + 4$

Question 250: C

This is a fourth order polynomial, which you aren't expected to be able to factorise at GCSE. This is where looking at the options makes your life a lot easier. In all of them, opening the bracket on the right side involves making $(y \pm 1)^4$ on the left side, i.e. the answers are hinting that $(y \pm 1)^4$ is the solution to the fourth order polynomial.

Since there are negative terms in the equations (e.g. $-4y^3$), the solution has to be:

$(y-1)^4 = y^4 - 4y^3 + 6y^2 - 4y + 1$

Therefore, $(y-1)^4 + 1 = x^5 + 7$

Thus, $y - 1 = (x^5 + 6)^{\frac{1}{4}}$

$y = 1 + (x^5 + 6)^{1/4}$

Question 251: A

Let the width of the television be 4x and the height of the television be 3x.

Then by Pythagoras: $(4x)^2 + (3x)^2 = 50^2$

Simplify: $25x^2 = 2500$

Thus: $x = 10$. Therefore: the screen is 30 inches by 40 inches, i.e. the area is 1,200 inches^2.

Question 252: C

Square both sides to give: $1 + \dfrac{3}{x^2} = (y^5 + 1)^2$

Multiply out: $\dfrac{3}{x^2} = (y^{10} + 2y^5 + 1) - 1$

Thus: $x^2 = \dfrac{3}{y^{10} + 2y^5}$

Therefore: $x = \sqrt{\dfrac{3}{y^{10} + 2y^5}}$

Question 253: C

The easiest way is to double the first equation and triple the second to get:

$6x - 10y = 20 \ and \ 6x + 6y = 39$.

Subtract the first from the second to give: $16y = 19$,

Therefore, $y = \dfrac{19}{16}$.

Substitute back into the first equation to give $x = \frac{85}{16}$.

Question 254: C

This is fairly straightforward; the first inequality is the easier one to work with: B and D and E violate it, so we just need to check A and C in the second inequality.

C: $1^3 - 2^2 < 3$, but A: $2^3 - 1^2 > 3$

Question 255: B

Whilst this can be done graphically, it's quicker to do algebraically (because the second equation is not as easy to sketch). Intersections occur where the curves have the same coordinates.

Thus: $x + 4 = 4x^2 + 5x + 5$

Simplify: $4x^2 + 4x + 1 = 0$

Factorise: $(2x + 1)(2x + 1) = 0$

Thus, the two graphs only intersect once at $x = -\dfrac{1}{2}$

Question 256: D

It's better to do this algebraically as the equations are easy to work with and you would need to sketch very accurately to get the answer. Intersections occur where the curves have the same coordinates. Thus: $x^3 = x$
$x^3 - x = 0$

Thus: $x(x^2 - 1) = 0$

Spot the 'difference between two squares': $x(x + 1)(x - 1) = 0$

Thus there are 3 intersections: at $x = 0, 1 \ and - 1$

Question 257: E

Note that the line is the hypotenuse of a right angled triangle with one side unit length and one side of length ½.

By Pythagoras, $\left(\dfrac{1}{2}\right)^2 + 1^2 = x^2$

Thus, $x^2 = \dfrac{1}{4} + 1 = \dfrac{5}{4}$

$x = \sqrt{\dfrac{5}{4}} = \dfrac{\sqrt{5}}{\sqrt{4}} = \dfrac{\sqrt{5}}{2}$

Question 258: D

We can eliminate z from equation (1) and (2) by multiplying equation (1) by 3 and adding it to equation (2):

3x + 3y – 3z = -3	Equation (1) multiplied by 3
2x – 2y +3z = 8	Equation (2) then add both equations
5x + y = 5	We label this as equation (4)

Now we must eliminate the same variable z from another pair of equations by using equation (1) and (3):

2x + 2y – 2z = -2	Equation (1) multiplied by 2
2x – y + 2z = 9	Equation (3) then add both equations
4x + y = 7	We label this as equation (5)

We now use both equations (4) and (5) to obtain the value of x:

5x + y = 5	Equation (4)
- 4x - y = -7	Equation (5) multiplied by -1
x = -2	

Substitute x back in to calculate y:

4x + y = 7

4(-2) + y = 7

$-8 + y = 7$

$y = 15$

Substitute x and y back in to calculate z:

$x + y - z = -1$

$-2 + 15 - z = -1$

$13 - z = -1$

$-z = -14$

$z = 14$

Thus: $x = -2$, $y = 15$, $z = 14$

Question 259: D

This is one of the easier maths questions. Take 3a as a factor to give:

$3a(a^2 - 10a + 25) = 3a(a - 5)(a - 5) = 3a(a - 5)^2$

Question 260: B

Note that 12 is the Lowest Common Multiple of 3 and 4. Thus:

$-3 (4x + 3y) = -3 (48)$ Multiply each side by -3

$4 (3x + 2y) = 4 (34)$ Multiply each side by 4

$-12x - 9y = -144$

$\underline{12x + 8y = 136}$ Add together

$-y = -8$

$y = 8$

Substitute y back in:

$4x + 3y = 48$

$4x + 3(8) = 48$

$4x + 24 = 48$

$4x = 24$

$x = 6$

Question 261: E

Don't be fooled, this is an easy question, just obey BODMAS and don't skip steps.

$$\frac{-(25 - 28)^2}{-36 + 14} = \frac{-(-3)^2}{-22}$$

This gives: $\dfrac{-(9)}{-22} = \dfrac{9}{22}$

Question 262: E

Since there are 26 possible letters for each of the 3 letters in the license plate, and there are 10 possible numbers (0-9) for each of the 3 numbers in the same plate, then the number of license plates would be:

$(26) \times (26) \times (26) \times (10) \times (10) \times (10) = 17,576,000$

Question 263: B

Expand the brackets to give: $4x^2 - 12x + 9 = 0$.

Factorise: $(2x - 3)(2x - 3) = 0$.

Thus, only one solution exists, x = 1.5.

Note that you could also use the fact that the discriminant, $b^2 - 4ac = 0$ to get the answer.

Question 264: C

$$= \left(x^2\right)^{\frac{1}{2}} (y^{-3})^{\frac{1}{2}}$$

$$= x^{\frac{1}{4}} y^{-\frac{3}{2}} = \frac{x^{\frac{1}{4}}}{y^{\frac{3}{2}}}$$

Question 265: A

Let x, y, and z represent the rent for the 1-bedroom, 2-bedroom, and 3-bedroom flats, respectively. We can write 3 different equations: 1 for the rent, 1 for the repairs, and the last one for the statement that the 3-bedroom unit costs twice as much as the 1-bedroom unit.

(1) $x + y + z = 1240$

(2) $0.1x + 0.2y + 0.3z = 276$

(3) $z = 2x$

Substitute $z = 2x$ in both of the two other equations to eliminate z:

(4) $x + y + 2x = 3x + y = 1240$

(5) $0.1x + 0.2y + 0.3(2x) = 0.7x + 0.2y = 276$

$-2(3x + y) = -2(1240)$	Multiply each side of (4) by -2
$10(0.7x + 0.2y) = 10(276)$	Multiply each side of (5) by 10
(6) $-6x - 2y = -2480$	Add these 2 equations
(7) $\underline{7x + 2y = 2760}$	
$x = 280$	
$z = 2(280) = 560$	Because $z = 2x$
$280 + y + 560 = 1240$	Because $x + y + z = 1240$
$y = 400$	

Thus the units rent for £ 280, £ 400, £ 560 per week respectively.

Question 266: C

Following BODMAS:

$$= 5\left[5(6^2 - 5 \times 3) + 400^{\frac{1}{2}}\right]^{1/3} + 7$$

$$= 5\left[5(36 - 15) + 20\right]^{\frac{1}{3}} + 7$$

$$= 5\left[5(21) + 20\right]^{\frac{1}{3}} + 7$$

$$= 5\left(105 + 20\right)^{\frac{1}{3}} + 7$$

$$= 5\left(125\right)^{\frac{1}{3}} + 7$$

$$= 5\left(5\right) + 7$$

$$= 25 + 7 = 32$$

Question 267: B

Consider a triangle formed by joining the centre to two adjacent vertices. Six similar triangles can be made around the centre – thus, the central angle is 60 degrees. Since the two lines forming the triangle are of equal length, we have 6 identical equilateral triangles in the hexagon.

Now split the triangle in half and apply Pythagoras' theorem:

$1^2 = 0.5^2 + h^2$

Thus, $h = \sqrt{\dfrac{3}{4}} = \dfrac{\sqrt{3}}{2}$

Thus, the area of the triangle is: $\dfrac{1}{2}bh = \dfrac{1}{2} \times 1 \times \dfrac{\sqrt{3}}{2} = \dfrac{\sqrt{3}}{4}$

Therefore, the area of the hexagon is: $\dfrac{\sqrt{3}}{4} \times 6 = \dfrac{3\sqrt{3}}{2}$

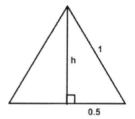

Question 268: B

Let x be the width and x+19 be the length.

Thus, the area of a rectangle is $x(x + 19) = 780$.

Therefore:

$x^2 + 19x - 780 = 0$

$(x - 20)(x + 39) = 0$

$x - 20 = 0$ or $x + 39 = 0$

$x = 20$ or $x = -39$

Since length can never be a negative number, we disregard $x = -39$ and use $x = 20$ instead.

Thus, the width is 20 metres and the length is 39 metres.

Question 269: B

The quickest way to solve is by trial and error, substituting the provided options. However, if you're keen to do this algebraically, you can do the following:

Start by setting up the equations: Perimeter $= 2L + 2W = 34$

Thus: $L + W = 17$

Using Pythagoras: $L^2 + W^2 = 13^2$

Since $L + W = 17$, $W = 17 - L$

Therefore: $L^2 + (17 - L)^2 = 169$

$L^2 + 289 - 34L + L^2 = 169$

$2L^2 - 34L + 120 = 0$

$L^2 - 17L + 60 = 0$

$(L - 5)(L - 12) = 0$

Thus: $L = 5$ and $L = 12$

And: $W = 12$ and $W = 5$

Question 270: C

Multiply both sides by 8: $4(3x - 5) + 2(x + 5) = 8(x + 1)$

Remove brackets: $12x - 20 + 2x + 10 = 8x + 8$

Simplify: $14x - 10 = 8x + 8$

Add 10: $14x = 8x + 18$

Subtract 8x: $6x = 18$

Therefore: $x = 3$

Question 271: C

Recognise that 1.742 x 3 is 5.226. Now, the original equation simplifies to:

$$= \frac{3 \times 10^6 + 3 \times 10^5}{10^{10}}$$

$$= 3 \times 10^{-4} + 3 \times 10^{-5} = 3.3 \times 10^{-4}$$

Question 272: A

$$Area = \frac{(2 + \sqrt{2})(4 - \sqrt{2})}{2}$$

$$= \frac{8 - 2\sqrt{2} + 4\sqrt{2} - 2}{2}$$

$$= \frac{6 + 2\sqrt{2}}{2}$$

$$= 3 + \sqrt{2}$$

Question 273: C

Square both sides: $\frac{4}{x} + 9 = (y - 2)^2$

$$\frac{4}{x} = (y - 2)^2 - 9$$

Cross Multiply: $\frac{x}{4} = \frac{1}{(y - 2)^2 - 9}$

$$x = \frac{4}{y^2 - 4y + 4 - 9}$$

Factorise: $x = \frac{4}{y^2 - 4y - 5}$

$$x = \frac{4}{(y + 1)(y - 5)}$$

Question 274: D

Set up the equation: $5x - 5 = 0.5 (6x + 2)$

$$10x - 10 = 6x + 2$$

$$4x = 12$$

$$x = 3$$

Question 275: C

Round numbers appropriately: $\frac{55 + (\frac{9}{4})^2}{\sqrt{900}} = \frac{55 + \frac{81}{16}}{30}$

81 rounds to 80 to give: $\frac{55 + 5}{30} = \frac{60}{30} = 2$

Question 276: D

There are three outcomes from choosing the type of cheese in the crust. For each of the additional toppings to possibly add, there are 2 outcomes: 1 to include and another not to include a certain topping, for each of the 7 toppings

Thus, the number of different kinds of pizza is: $3 \times 2 \times 2 \times 2 \times 2 \times 2 \times 2 \times 2 = 3 \times 2^7$

$= 3 \times 128 = 384$

Question 277: A

Although it is possible to do this algebraically, by far the easiest way is via trial and error. The clue that you shouldn't attempt it algebraically is the fact that rearranging the first equation to make x or y the subject leaves you with a difficult equation to work with (e.g. $x = \sqrt{1 - y^2}$) when you try to substitute in the second.

An exceptionally good student might notice that the equations are symmetric in x and y, i.e. the solution is when

$x = y$. Thus $2x^2 = 1$ and $2x = \sqrt{2}$ which gives $\dfrac{\sqrt{2}}{2}$ as the answer.

Question 278: C

If two shapes are congruent, then they are the same size and shape. Thus, congruent objects can be rotations and mirror images of each other. The two triangles in E are indeed congruent (SAS). Congruent objects must, by definition, have the same angles.

Question 279: B

Rearrange the equation: $x^2 + x - 6 \geq 0$

Factorise: $(x + 3)(x - 2) \geq 0$

Remember that this is a quadratic inequality so requires a quick sketch to ensure you don't make a silly mistake with which way the sign is. Thus, $y = 0$ when $x = 2$ and $x = -3$. $y > 0$ when $x > 2$ or $x < -3$. Thus, the solution is: $x \leq -3 \ and \ x \geq 2$.

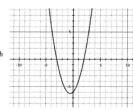

Question 280: B

Using Pythagoras: $a^2 + b^2 = x^2$

Since the triangle is equilateral: $a = b, \ so \ 2a^2 = x^2$

Area $= \dfrac{1}{2}base \ x \ height = \dfrac{1}{2}a^2$. From above, $a^2 = \dfrac{x^2}{2}$

Thus the area $= \dfrac{1}{2}x\dfrac{x^2}{2} = \dfrac{x^2}{4}$

Question 281: A

If X and Y are doubled, the value of Q increases by 4. Halving the value of A reduces this to 2. Finally, tripling the value of B reduces this to ⅔, i.e. the value decreases by ⅓.

Question 282: C

The quickest way to do this is to sketch the curves. This requires you to factorise both equations by completing the square:

$x^2 - 2x + 3 = (x-1)^2 + 2$

$x^2 - 6x - 10 = (x-3)^2 - 19$ Thus, the first equation has a turning point at (1, 2) and doesn't cross the x-axis. The second equation has a turning point at (3, -19) and crosses the x-axis twice.

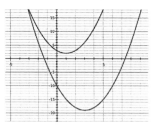

Question 283: C

Segment area $= \frac{60}{360}\pi r^2 = \frac{1}{6}\pi r^2$

$\frac{x}{\sin 30°} = \frac{2r}{\sin 60°}$

$x = \frac{2r}{\sqrt{3}}$

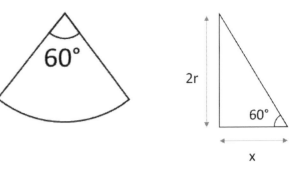

Total triangle area $= 2 \times \frac{1}{2} \times \frac{2r}{\sqrt{3}} \times 2r = \frac{4r^2}{\sqrt{3}}$

Proportion covered: $\frac{\frac{1}{6}\pi r^2}{\frac{4r^2}{\sqrt{3}}} = \frac{\sqrt{3}\pi}{24} \approx 23\%$

Question 284: B

$(2r)^2 = r^2 + x^2$

$3r^2 = x^2$

$x = \sqrt{3}r$

$Total\ height = 2r + x = (2 + \sqrt{3})r$

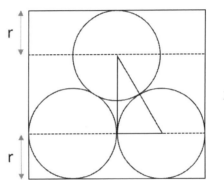
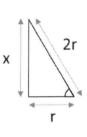

Question 285: A

$V = \frac{1}{3}h \times \text{base area}$

Therefore base area must be equal if h and V are the same

Internal angle $= 180° - $ external ; external $= 360°/6 = 60°$

giving internal angle $120°$

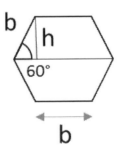

Hexagon is two trapezia of height h where: $\frac{b}{\sin 90°} = \frac{h}{\sin 60°}$

$h = \frac{\sqrt{3}}{2}b$

Trapezium area $= \frac{(2b + b)\sqrt{3}}{2}b = \frac{3\sqrt{3}}{4}b^2$

Total hexagon area $= \frac{3\sqrt{3}}{2}b^2$

So from equal volumes: $a^2 = \frac{3\sqrt{3}}{2}b^2$

Ratio: $\sqrt{\frac{3\sqrt{3}}{2}}$

Question 286: C

A cube has 6 sides so the area of 9 cm cube = 6 x 9^2

9 cm cube splits into 3 cm cubes.

Area of 3 cm cubes = 3^3 x 6 x 3^2

$$\frac{6 \times 3^2 \times 3^3}{6 \times 3^2 \times 3^2} = 3$$

Question 287: ~~E~~ C

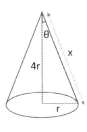

$$x^2 = (4r)^2 + r^2$$
$$x = \sqrt{17}r$$
$$\frac{\sqrt{17}r}{\sin 90°} = \frac{r}{\sin \theta}$$
$$\theta = \sin^{-1}\left(\frac{1}{\sqrt{17}}\right)$$

Question 288: C

0 to 200 is 180 degrees so: $\dfrac{\theta}{180} = \dfrac{70}{200}$

$$\theta = \frac{7 \times 180}{20} = 63°$$

Question 289: C

Since the rhombi are similar, the ratio of angles = 1

Length scales with square root of area so length B = $\sqrt{10}$ length A

$$\frac{angle\ A \big/ angle\ B}{length\ A \big/ length\ B} = \frac{1}{\sqrt{10}\big/1} = \frac{1}{\sqrt{10}}$$

Question 290: E

$$y = ln(2x^2)$$
$$e^y = 2x^2$$
$$x = \sqrt{\frac{e^y}{2}}$$

As the input is -x, the inverse function must be $f(x) = -\sqrt{\dfrac{e^y}{2}}$

Question 291: C

$log_8(x)$ and $log_{10}(x) < 0$; $x^2 < 1$; $\sin(x) \le 1$ and $1 < e^x < 2.72$

So e^x is largest over this range

Question 292: C

$$x \propto \sqrt{z^3}$$
$$\sqrt{2^3} = 2\sqrt{2}$$

Question 293: A

The area of the shaded part, that is the difference between the area of the larger and smaller circles, is three times the area of the smaller so: $\pi r^2 - \pi x^2 = 3\pi x^2$. From this, we can see that the area of the larger circle, radius x, must be 4x the smaller one so: $4\pi r^2 = \pi x^2$

$$4r^2 = x^2$$
$$x = 2r$$

The gap is $x - r = 2r - r = r$

Question 294: D

$$x^2 + 3x - 4 \ge 0$$
$$(x - 1)(x + 4) \ge 0$$

Hence, $x - 1 \ge 0$ or $x + 4 \ge 0$

So $x \ge 1$ or $x \ge -4$

Question 295: C

$$\frac{4}{3}\pi r^3 = \pi r^2$$

$$\frac{4}{3}r = 1$$

$$r = \frac{3}{4}$$

Question 296: B

When $x^2 = \frac{1}{x}; x = 1$

When $x > 1, x^2 > 1, \frac{1}{x} < 1$

When $x < 1, x^2 < 1, \frac{1}{x} > 1$

Range for $\frac{1}{x}$ is $x > 0$

Non-inclusive so: $0 < x < 1$

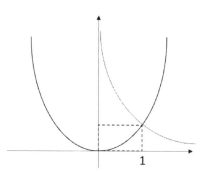

Question 297: A

Don't be afraid of how difficult this initially looks. If you follow the pattern, you get (e-e) which = 0. Anything multiplied by 0 gives zero.

Question 298: C

For two vectors to be perpendicular their scalar product must be equal to 0.

Hence, $\begin{pmatrix} -1 \\ 6 \end{pmatrix} \cdot \begin{pmatrix} 2 \\ k \end{pmatrix} = 0$

$\therefore -2 + 6k = 0$

$k = \frac{1}{3}$

Question 299: C

The point, q, in the plane meets the perpendicular line from the plane to the point p.

$q = -3i + j + \lambda_1(i + 2j)$

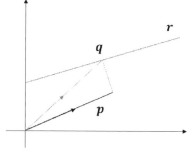

$\vec{PQ} = -3i + j + \lambda_1(i + 2j) + 4i + 5j$

$= \begin{pmatrix} -7 + \lambda_1 \\ -4 + 2\lambda_1 \end{pmatrix}$

PQ is perpendicular to the plane r therefore the dot product of $\vec{PQ}$ and a vector within the plane must be 0.

$\begin{pmatrix} -7 + \lambda_1 \\ -4 + 2\lambda_1 \end{pmatrix} \cdot \begin{pmatrix} 1 \\ 2 \end{pmatrix} = 0$

$\therefore -7 + \lambda_1 - 8 + 4 + \lambda_1 = 0$

$\lambda_1 = 3$

$\vec{PQ} = \begin{pmatrix} -4 \\ 2 \end{pmatrix}$

The perpendicular distance from the plane to point p is therefore the modulus of the vector joining the two $\vec{PQ}$:

$|\vec{PQ}| = \sqrt{(-4)^2 + 2^2} = \sqrt{20} = 2\sqrt{5}$

Question 300: E

$-1 + 3\mu = -7 \; ; \mu = -2$

$2 + 4\lambda + 2\mu = 2 \; \therefore \; \lambda = 1$

$3 + \lambda + \mu = k \; \therefore \; k = 2$

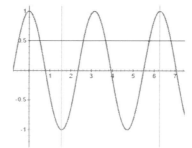

Question 301: E

$\sin\left(\dfrac{\pi}{2} - 2\theta\right) = \cos(2\theta)$

Root solution to $\cos(\theta) = 0.5$

$\theta = \dfrac{\pi}{3}$

Solution to $\cos(2\theta) = 0.5$

$\theta = \dfrac{\pi}{6}$

Largest solution within range is: $2\pi - \dfrac{\pi}{6} = \dfrac{(12-1)\pi}{6} = \dfrac{11\pi}{6}$

Question 302: A

$\cos^4(x) - \sin^4(x) \equiv \left\{\cos^2(x) - \sin^2(x)\right\}\left\{\cos^2(x) + \sin^2(x)\right\}$

From difference of two squares, then using Pythagorean identity $\cos^2(x) + \sin^2(x) = 1$

$\cos^4(x) - \sin^4(x) \equiv \cos^2(x) - \sin^2(x)$

But double angle formula says: $\cos(A + B) = \cos(A)\cos(B) - \sin(A)\sin(B)$

$\therefore \; if \; A = B, \cos(2A) = \cos(A)\cos(A) - \sin(A)\sin(A)$

$= \cos^2(A) - \sin^2(A)$

So, $\cos^4(x) - \sin^4(x) \equiv \cos(2x)$

Question 303: C

Factorise: $(x + 1)(x + 2)(2x - 1)(x^2 + 2) = 0$

Three real roots at $x = -1, x = -2, x = 0.5$ and two imaginary roots at 2i and -2i

Question 304: C

An arithmetic sequence has constant difference d so the sum increases by d more each time:

$u_n = u_1 + (n - 1)d$

$\displaystyle\sum_1^n u_n = \dfrac{n}{2}\{2u_1 + (n - 1)d\}$

$\displaystyle\sum_1^8 u_n = \dfrac{8}{2}\{4 + (8 - 1)3\} = 100$

Question 305: E

$\dbinom{n}{k}2^{n-k}(-x)^k = \dbinom{5}{2}2^{5-2}(-x)^2$

$= 10 \times 2^3 x^2 = 80x^2$

Question 306: A

Having already thrown a 6 is irrelevant. A fair die has equal probability $P = \dfrac{1}{6}$ for every throw.

For three throws: $P(6 \cap 6 \cap 6) = \left(\frac{1}{6}\right)^3 = \frac{1}{216}$

Question 307: D

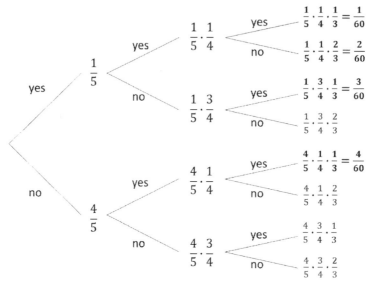

Total probability is sum of all probabilities:
$$= P(Y \cap Y \cap Y) + P(Y \cap Y \cap N) + P(Y \cap N \cap Y) + P(N \cap Y \cap Y)$$
$$= \frac{1}{60} + \frac{2}{60} + \frac{3}{60} + \frac{4}{60} = \frac{10}{60} = \frac{1}{6}$$

Question 308: C
$$P\left[(A \cup B)'\right] = 1 - P[(A \cup B)]$$
$$= 1 - \{P(A) + P(B) - P(A \cap B)\}$$
$$= 1 - \frac{2 + 6 - 1}{8} = \frac{3}{8}$$

Question 309: D
$$\frac{dy}{dx} = x \cdot 4(x + 3)^3 + 1 \cdot (x + 3)^4$$
Using the product rule:
$$= 4x(x + 3)^3 + (x + 3)(x + 3)^3$$
$$= (5x + 3)(x + 3)^3$$

Question 310: A C
$$\int_1^2 \frac{2}{x^2}dx = \int_1^2 2x^{-2}dx =$$
$$\left[\frac{2x^{-1}}{-1}\right]_1^2 = \left[\frac{-2}{x}\right]_1^2$$
$$= \frac{-2}{2} - \frac{-2}{1} = -1$$

Question 311: D
Express $\dfrac{5i}{1 + 2i}$ in the form $a + b\square i$
$$\frac{5i}{1 + 2i} \cdot \frac{1 - 2i}{1 - 2i}$$
$$= \frac{5i + 10}{1 + 4} \quad \frac{5i + 10}{5}$$
$$= i + 2$$

Question 312: B

$7\log_a(2) - 3\log_a(12) + 5\log_a(3)$

$7\log_a(2) = \log_a(2^7) = \log_a(128)$

$3\log_a(12) = \log_a(1728)$

$5\log_a(3) = \log_a(243)$

This gives: $\log_a(128) - \log_a(1728) + \log_a(243)$

$= \log_a\left(\dfrac{128 \times 243}{1728}\right) = \log_a(18)$

Question 313: E

Functions of the form quadratic over quadratic have a horizontal asymptote.

Divide each term by the highest order in the polynomial i.e. x^2:

$$\frac{2x^2 - x + 3}{x^2 + x - 2} = \frac{2 - \dfrac{1}{x} + \dfrac{3}{x^2}}{1 + \dfrac{1}{x} - \dfrac{2}{x^2}}$$

$$\lim_{x \to \infty} \left(\frac{2 - \dfrac{1}{x} + \dfrac{3}{x^2}}{1 + \dfrac{1}{x} - \dfrac{2}{x^2}}\right) = \frac{2}{1} \ i.e. \ y \to 2$$

So, the asymptote is $y = 2$

Question 314: A

$1 - 3e^{-x} = e^x - 3$

$4 = e^x + 3e^{-x} = \dfrac{(e^x)^2}{e^x} + \dfrac{3}{e^x} = \dfrac{(e^x)^2 + 3}{e^x}$

This is a quadratic equation in (e^x): $(e^x)^2 - 4(e^x) + 3 = 0$

$(e^x - 3)(e^x - 1) = 0$

So $e^x = 3, x = ln(3)$ or $e^x = 1, x = 0$

Question 315: D

Rearrange into the format: $(x + a)^2 + (y + b)^2 = r^2$

$(x - 3)^2 + (y + 4)^2 - 25 = 12$

$(x - 3)^2 + (y + 4)^2 = 47$

$\therefore r = \sqrt{47}$

Question 316: C

$\sin(-x) = -\sin(x)$

$\int_0^a 2\sin(-x)dx = -2\int_0^a \sin(x)dx = -2[\cos(x)]_0^a = \cos(a) - 1$

Solve $\cos(a) - 1 = 0 \ \therefore a = 2k\pi$

Or simply the integral of any whole period of sin(x) = 0 i.e. $a = 2k\pi$

Question 317: E

$$\frac{2x + 3}{(x - 2)(x - 3)^2} = \frac{A}{(x - 2)} + \frac{B}{(x - 3)} + \frac{C}{(x - 3)^2}$$

$2x + 3 = A(x - 3)^2 + B(x - 2)(x - 3) + C(x - 2)$

When $x = 3, (x - 3) = 0$, $C = 9$

When $x = 2, (x - 2) = 0, A = 7$

$2x + 3 = 7(x - 3)^2 + B(x - 2)(x - 3) + 9(x - 2)$

For completeness: Equating coefficients of x^2 on either side: $0 = 7 + B$ which gives: $B = -7$

END OF SECTION

Final Advice

Arrive well rested, well fed and well hydrated

The ECAA is an intensive test, so make sure you're ready for it. Ensure you get a good night's sleep before the exam (there is little point cramming) and don't miss breakfast. If you're taking water into the exam then make sure you've been to the toilet before so you don't have to leave during the exam. Make sure you're well rested and fed in order to be at your best!

Move on

If you're struggling, move on. Every question has equal weighting and there is no negative marking. In the time it takes to answer on hard question, you could gain three times the marks by answering the easier ones. Be smart to score points- especially in section 1B where some questions are far easier than others.

Make Notes on your Essay

You may be asked questions on your ECAA essay at the interview. Given that there is likely to be several weeks between the test and interview, it is imperative that you make short notes on the essay title and your main arguments after the essay.

Afterword

Remember that the route to a high score is your approach and practice. Don't fall into the trap that "*you can't prepare for the ECAA*"– this could not be further from the truth. With knowledge of the test, some useful time-saving techniques and plenty of practice you can dramatically boost your score.

Work hard, never give up and do yourself justice.

Good luck!

Acknowledgements

I would like to express my sincerest thanks to the many people who helped make this book possible, especially the Oxbridge Tutors who shared their expertise in compiling the huge number of questions and answers.

Rohan

About UniAdmissions

UniAdmissions is an educational consultancy that specialises in supporting **applications to Medical School and to Oxbridge**.

Every year, we work with hundreds of applicants and schools across the UK. From free resources to our *Ultimate Guide Books* and from intensive courses to bespoke individual tuition – with a team of **300 Expert Tutors** and a proven track record, it's easy to see why UniAdmissions is the **UK's number one admissions company**.

To find out more about our support like intensive **ECAA tuition** check out www.uniadmissions.co.uk/ECAA

Printed in Great Britain
by Amazon